THE ANONYMOUS LEADER

An Unambitious
Pursuit of Influence

RALPH MAYHEW

In a time when it is easy to craft our own image and advance our leadership journey under our own steam, *The Anonymous Leader* is a timely reminder of the importance of humble, Christlike leadership.

Mark Sayers, Senior Leader Red Church,
author of Facing Leviathan, *and* Disappearing Church

The hardest person a leader will lead is himself or herself. In *The Anonymous Leader* my good friend and colleague Ralph Mayhew paints a beautiful picture of self-leadership modelled on the life of Jesus. This is no mere theory, but the distillation of lessons hard won by Ralph in everyday leadership environments, all based in timeless Biblical principles. I have seen first-hand Ralph live these principles out as he has built a thriving ministry and developed a continuous stream of servant-hearted leaders. Please read this book – and get it into the hands of anyone considering embarking on the leadership adventure!

Stu Cameron, Lead Minister Newlife Uniting Church, Gold Coast

Without doubt, the world always needs more and better leaders. However, this is especially so in our generation, which is currently facing unprecedented challenges and uncertainty. Ralph Mayhew's new book *The Anonymous Leader* is packed full of wisdom and insight for both emerging and experienced leaders. I highly recommend it!

Mark Conner, Senior Minister CityLife Church, Melbourne,
author of Transforming Your Church

This book should come with a warning label! Ralph Mayhew invites all who claim the name 'leader', to consider the 'upside down' approach to acting in a way that serves, develops and releases others to their potential. To put aside the unhealthy aspects of ambition and take up the silent, diligent, and often costly aspects of true Christ-like leadership. This book not only challenges how leadership is being experienced now, it also shows how it can be done differently and diligently. Read with care! Leadership is more grey than black and white, more art than science, more pathway than highway. In this book Ralph Mayhew navigates the paradox of a desire for leadership greatness while navigating the importance of anonymity and humility. He skilfully unpacks and repacks a toolkit that will serve leaders now and leaders next.

Rohan Dredge, Senior Pastor Discovery Church, leadership blogger

I first met Ralph in 2010 when he undertook the Arrow Program and have watched his progress since that time. I was privileged to see an early draft of *The Anonymous Leader* and I have to admit that I am surprised by how much I enjoyed reading the final version. In an age when way too many leaders are getting caught up in rock star Christianity, Ralph is pointing us in the right direction. This is a book full of wisdom for younger leaders and some timely reminders for those of us further down the road.

Julian Dunham, Emerging Leaders Program Director,
Arrow Leadership Australia

No re-appraisal could be more timely as we recover from the infliction of grandiose, heroic models of leadership. In this book, Ralph has symptomised a return to the simple qualities of character, call and commitment, iced with Christlike humility. *The Anonymous Leader* is a must-read primer for those setting out on the journey, and a pointed reminder for those for whom the leadership path is well trod.

Craig Bailey, Director of Leadership Uniting College,
Adelaide College of Divinity

I recommend *The Anonymous Leader* as a valuable book that takes the reader to the very heart of leadership – who the leader is, their character and credibility. It illustrates how leadership has crucial purposes that surpass mere personal ambition. It will prompt emerging and seasoned leaders to develop their self-understanding and consequently increase their influence.

Rev Dr Dean Brookes, Leadership coach and mentor,
Uniting Church Minister

Ralph, in *The Anonymous Leader*, has captured the true essence of Christian leadership. He has researched well and the honesty of the personal journey truly challenged and encouraged me to continue to be a lifelong learner. The key insights I gleaned around Biblical leadership reminded me again of both the privilege and responsibility leaders carry in serving others well. I recommend *The Anonymous Leader* as a must-read for all leaders at every level of experience.

Rick Wright, Senior Pastor Kardinia Church, Geelong

I am thrilled to endorse Ralph Mayhew's *The Anonymous Leader* as a book that speaks right to the heart of modern-day issues for the Christian leader. Leaders today are seeking more than just leadership theory. Ralph's authentic and insightful look at leadership is born out of hard-learnt leadership lessons. Oh and by the way, like me you may just find yourself lapping up the excellent leadership theory.

Carl Mutzelburg, Lead Pastor Catalyst Church, Ipswich, QLD

Knowing Ralph well, I can affirm this book has been written out of his authentic, genuine love for Jesus and desire to make him known to others. Ralph is a humble and gifted leader and we all would be wise to read and engage with *The Anonymous Leader*. In a time when Australian leadership writing and content is sparse, *The Anonymous Leader* fills an important gap in developing leaders – pointing them to a deeper intimacy with Jesus.

Mike Stevens, State Youth and Young Adults Facilitator, South Australia

The Anonymous Leader addresses the topic of leadership in a way that is desperately needed within the church. Ralph provides a fresh take on this topic by helping us understand what it means to allow God to lead in and through us. *The Anonymous Leader* provides insightful challenge to the veteran leader and important guidance to those beginning to accept the responsibility of leading others. This is a must-read for all leaders.

Dale Braswell, Lead Pastor LifePoint Church in Lynnwood, WA, USA

Ralph has learned and refined these principles during many years of local church leadership. Readers will find themselves easily identifying with Ralph's stories and will come away with tools and insights to make a difference in their context. This book is a fantastic resource to develop the skills and heart God is looking for in passionate leadership.

Geoff Snook, Senior Pastor The Lakes Church, Cairns

Amongst the plethora of leadership material on my bookshelves, there is very little material that both challenges the seasoned leader and builds the right foundations for a novice, amateur leader at the same time. This book successfully does both: whilst providing great moments of introspection for leaders of great experience, it is also a book that every young, first-time or new leader must read. However, the true authority comes from Ralph Mayhew himself, who has lived and breathed every principle and leadership trait in this book long before a word of the manuscript was written. A must-read for all leaders.

Michael Hands, Youth Pastor Newlife Uniting Church, Gold Coast

Ralph Mayhew's *The Anonymous Leader* is a work which reflects his own journey to become a God-honouring leader. His passion to honour Christ in how he leads is refreshing and guarantees authentic insights from his personal learnings. Leadership challenges will increase as we get deeper into this 21st century, and this book will be a reference manual that will inspire a new generation of leaders. It's a must-read.

Phillip Mutzelburg, President of Acts 2 Alliance

The Anonymous Leader beautifully captures the essence of the paradigm of Kingdom. Ralph has placed in your hands an invitation for you to shepherd the next generation of revivalists toward developing their leadership from Heaven's perspective.

Mark Appleyard, Lead Pastor Crossroads Church, Weddington, NC, USA

The Anonymous Leader is birthed out of a life of leadership from the author Ralph Mayhew. Real personal stories, cemented in biblical principles that every potential leader or already established leader could see themselves part of. This book seeks to challenge the very core of the person and get them to ask themselves a question: is this about me? Or about Jesus and the people I have been charged to lead? As you journey through this incredible book you will be challenged to take an inward look into your outward leadership.

Neil Milton, Senior Pastor Liberty Family Church, Healesville

Nothing exposes our motives more than when we are given the opportunity to lead. *The Anonymous Leader* has challenged me to ask, 'Am I using the platform God has given me to build my own following or to lead others to be influenced by God?' Read this book and be prepared to be challenged. Ralph Mayhew weaves his own leadership experiences with his wide interactions with many leaders and authors to teach us what Christian leadership is all about – anonymity. He paints vivid pictures from the scriptures to call us to a leadership that is not about us. He shows how we can use the platform God has given us for the benefit of others. Since I first met Ralph, he has been an anonymous leader who raises up anonymous leaders. You will love reading this book. I hope it is read widely. We need the kind of leaders Ralph inspires us to become.

Jonathan Stark, Senior Pastor Wodonga District Baptist Church

The Anonymous Leader is an important contribution to the world of leadership wisdom. It speaks not of a leader's more obvious charismatic gifts, but of their humility and inner life. Ralph's thoughts will be challenging (in a good way) to everyone who has ever felt called to lead anything.

Melissa Lipsett, Executive Minister Newlife Uniting Church, Gold Coast

I always look forward to a coffee with Ralph to listen to his heart for God and the wisdom that he has been given. His insights are essential for those who want to go deeper in raising up disciples who make disciples.

Jon Owen, National Director UNOH, author of Muddy Spirituality

Ralph Mayhew has written a deep and challenging book that defines what integrity means for the Christian leader. Ralph lives out what he has written and he offers readers a pathway for what is often a complex journey of mixed motives. I highly recommend it.

Rev Alan Robinson, Presbytery Minister South Moreton Presbytery, Uniting Church, QLD

Ralph is a leader who possesses a rare gift and insight to see things differently. This is evidenced by Ralph's forward-thinking paradigm of authentic faith-based leadership as revealed in *The Anonymous Leader*.

Brad Beer, Physiotherapist, Author, Founder and CEO of POGO Physio

There has never been a more important time than the present for God's leaders to understand what it means to truly hear that call of Jesus saying, 'Come, follow me.' In a world where culture has engrained in each of us a desire to be known, where the pursuit of fame and acclaim stand as giants taunting the heart of a modern leader, Ralph Mayhew's *The Anonymous Leader* stands as a beacon of light in the darkness. A must-read for any leader seeking to see God's Kingdom come in a self-obsessed generation.

David Shepherd, Student Spiritual Development Facilitator, Concordia College and Associate Pastor

First Published in 2015 by Ralph Mayhew
www.ralphmayhew.com
www.theanonymousleader.com

© 2015 Ralph Mayhew

This title is also available as an ebook.
Visit www.amazon.com.

This title will also be available as an audio edition.
Visit www.amazon.com.

All enquiries should be made to the author at ralph@ralphmayhew.com

National Library of Australia Cataloguing-in-Publication entry:
Creator: Mayhew, Ralph, author.
Title: The anonymous leader: an unambitious pursuit of influence
ISBN: 9780994405593 (paperback)
Subjects: Leadership.
Leadership – Religious aspects.
Motivation (Psychology) – Religious aspects.
Self-actualization (Psychology) – Religious aspects.
Dewey Number: 658.4092

Edited by: Charlotte Duff
Interior Design by: Kerry Stacey
Cover Design by: Craig Hindman
Book production by: Michael Hanrahan Publishing
Printed in Australia by: McPherson's Printing

The listing of website references and resources does not imply publisher endorsement of the site's or author's entire contents. Groups and individuals are listed for informational purposes, and listing does not imply publisher endorsement of their activities.

Unless otherwise indicated, quotations from the Bible are in the author's own paraphrase. Scripture taken from the HOLY BIBLE, NEW INTERNATIONAL VERSION®. NIV®. Copyright © 1973, 1978, 1984 by International Bible Society. Used by permission of Zondervan. All rights reserved worldwide.

*This book is dedicated to Lyndal:
without your constant support, it would not exist.*

Thank you for always believing in me.

I love you with all my heart.

I wrote this book for you,
the potential Anonymous Leader.
My hope is that it will entice you to
give everything you have to the Cause of Christ,
to which you are called. May the words
you read enable you to hear God's Spirit whisper
to you, enriching your leadership and the
influence you bring to those you lead.

SPECIAL THANKS

I WANT TO thank and acknowledge the following people for their support in making what you hold in your hands possible.

To Lyndal, my amazing wife – without you I could not do or be who I am. Thanks for your patience, ideas, support and belief in me; I love doing life with you, you're my best friend. This is as much from you as it is from me.

To my beautiful daughter, Azaria – how blessed we are to have you. I've loved every single interruption as you invited me to play or cuddle instead of work. You make my heart full and my spirit happy.

To my parents – you sought to give me the best opportunities in life and I'm so grateful. Thanks, Mum, for introducing me to Jesus and always being there. I love you both very much.

To the 'Pipeline Crew' – you have taught me more about leadership than I have you. I deeply appreciate your eagerness to learn.

To the Newlife Leadership Team I lead with – you each cause me to lead better every day. And to Newlife Uniting Church for trusting me to lead and develop leaders. I love being the church with you. Also to 12two, the young adult community I lead and love. It is an absolute honour to lead you; you have taught me so much.

To those at Seymour Uniting Church during my season of ministry there – I value each of you dearly.

To my first church family in Melton Uniting Church – I would not have started leading as early as I did without your constant encouragement, belief and prayer.

To all my friends who believed I could write a book well before I thought I could – you know who you are. Thank you.

To every other leader, mentor, coach, manager and supervisor I have met along the way – you have sharpened my leadership edge. Without each of you, I would not be the leader I am.

To Jesus – in you I live and move and have my being. My gratitude will never satisfy the gift of grace you continue to give to me. May you use this book to do Your will in people's lives.

CONTENTS

Introduction **1**

Part I: The context
1. Of course you're a leader **9**
2. Defining leadership and anonymity **17**
3. Learning from John the Baptist **41**
4. Love or insanity? **57**

Part II: The platform
5. Cloaks and platforms **71**
6. Fencing in the platform **87**
7. Fencing in the platform for leaders and teams **115**
8. Understanding the work of the Holy Spirit **123**

Part III: The five foundational leadership components
9. Migrating passion into wisdom **131**
10. Building trust into integrity **149**
11. Ushering invincibility into humility **165**
12. Nurturing confidence into security **181**
13. Driving commitment into resilience **197**

Part IV: The cost
14. The trade-off **219**
15. Hearing your calling **229**
16. Embracing 'chair time' **239**

Epilogue **249**
Further resources **251**
Acknowledgements **262**
What's next? **263**
About the author **264**

INTRODUCTION

I WRESTLED WITH even writing this book. This book is about fading away and becoming nothing so Jesus Christ can become everything through your life and leadership. The irony in writing a book – having it published and having people buy it and read it – is that the opposite can occur. My name is now known by more people and my reputation increases. The platform upon which I stand is ironically elevated.

So I struggled for a long time about whether to write anything at all. On more than one occasion, I felt that merely creating this book was hypocritical to what the book calls us to.

But much prayer has gone into this book – before it was conceived, as it was being planned, and throughout the writing of it. Each step along the journey I have felt the impression of God on my spirit, so that this book – while penned by me – was inspired by Him.

This book is as much for me as it is for those who will read it. In writing, reading and editing it, God's Spirit has arrested me many times over inconsistencies in my leadership and areas in need of attention. I have grieved over mistakes I've made. I cannot tell some stories that belong to others and myself because of the pain associated with them. I even contemplated doing what other authors have done and replacing my name with 'Anonymous'.

This book is about me and the journey God has taken me on, but only because God might use the things He has used to shape my leadership to do the same for you. I wrote this for you, to help you improve your self-leadership and become a better leader. Leading ourselves is one of the greatest challenges in leadership. We rarely do what we want and constantly disappoint ourselves – and, although deeply apologetic, we continue to make the same mistakes. Be encouraged that you can change, because God will change you if you let Him.

The structure of this book is designed to lead you through a different framework of how to look at leadership and explore the implications of it.

PART I – The context

All leadership is understood in a context. Even in Christianity, our context can be too businesslike and not enough Bible-like. The chapters in this part establish the groundwork for exploring the context of Anonymous Leadership, which stands completely in contrast to ambitious leadership.

Anonymous Leadership is the positive, intentional influence offered to another for their benefit as they align themselves with the Cause you serve. Leading is not about you or your influence – it is about God influencing others through you and receiving the glory or credit because of it.

Ambition is not about determination or drive; indeed, both of these things are good. Rather, ambition as I refer to it in this book is about the self-seeking desire to promote and further yourself above the Cause you serve. The New Testament only uses the term 'ambition' to capture this idea of self-indulgent furtherance, and this is the way I too use it in this book.

We see the tension between ambition and anonymity lived out so powerfully in John the Baptist's life, and we explore this in chapter 3. John had a deep love for Jesus and the Kingdom of God that framed and empowered his leadership, providing us with a model of what Anonymous Leadership looks like.

PART II – The platform

Out of the context outlined in part I emerges the platform from which a leader leads. Leadership is not a right we have but an opportunity we are given – we are invited onto a platform provided by God, to influence people on His behalf. Many of the things we concern ourselves with in leadership need not be of concern if we rest in the assurance that God is behind us and our greatest action is to become transparent enough that those following us might see God's desires for their lives.

The platform is hemmed in by fences, much like an electric fence that you cross at your own peril. The four sides of the platform are vision, values, culture and heart. The Anonymous Leader leads freely within these four fences to ensure that the people are led with excellence and within the bounds of God's Kingdom.

These fences work equally for an individual leader, a leader you are wanting to empower and a whole team – anyone who seeks to lead for the Cause of Christ and the sake of the people.

PART III – The five foundational leadership components

Every leader who steps onto the platform to lead has five components to what they offer: passion, trust, invincibility, confidence and commitment. I call these 'components' rather than 'characteristics' because every person has many different characteristics, as does every leader, whereas a component is necessary for something to work. If a component of a cake is missing, the ingredients do not make a cake. If a component of an engine is missing, it doesn't run. Components are essential aspects that are required for something to be whole.

The task of the leader is to steward each of these components towards an anonymous expression of leadership, as follows:

- Passion is stewarded toward wisdom and away from recklessness.

- Trust is stewarded towards integrity and away from hypocrisy.
- Invincibility is stewarded towards humility and away from pride.
- Confidence is stewarded towards security and away from insecurity.
- Commitment is stewarded towards resilience and away from shallowness.

In successfully stewarding these five components toward anonymity, ambition is gradually removed from a leader's influence. This results in Christ being more clearly identified in the leadership that an Anonymous Leader offers.

PART IV – The cost

Stewarding the five components of leadership toward anonymity comes at a cost. The act of leading costs every leader, but it is essential to make sure the right cost is being paid. Failure to make great trade-offs – that is, trading the good for the great – can result in long-term losses for a leader, just as making great trade-offs can benefit a leader and those they lead for many years to come.

The greatest trade-off a leader can make is to surrender to the call of God on their life. Without first being called and then accepting the call, a leader cannot be sustained on the platform. The call is what enables a Christian leader to do what God asks of them and selflessly further the Cause of Christ.

The calling is essential to leadership, but without the spiritual discipline of meeting daily with God, our calling will dry up as the weight of it becomes overpowering. God called you to carry His influence to those He wants to lead. As you carry His influence, He carries you, sustaining you through all that leading others assaults you with.

Introduction

Can I be an Anonymous Leader?

This book is written for every person who would dare to ask this question.

This book is for those who are new to leadership and want to set themselves on a trajectory that ensures the greatness of their cause.

This book is written for leaders of leaders, who are charged with an incredible responsibility – to nurture, train, encourage, challenge and compel emerging leaders to become excellent.

This book is for those who hunger to lead so that the Cause of Christ increases as they decrease.

This book is for pastors to give to emerging leaders so they might have a reference point to lead from.

This book is for those leaders who are leading people but would never call themselves a leader.

This book is for those leaders who you know are leaders but haven't worked it out themselves yet. Perhaps you're the person to encourage them by giving them a copy.

This book is for those leaders thirsty for a refreshing exploration of what Christian leadership is.

ANONYMOUS LEADERSHIP IS ABOUT PUTTING ASIDE YOURSELF, YOUR AMBITIONS, YOUR VISIONS OF GRANDEUR, YOUR SECRET AGENDA OF WORLD DOMINATION, YOUR HUNGRY EGO, AND YOUR DESIRE FOR ACCLAIM AND RECOGNITION.

Jesus Christ – Leader, Saviour, Messiah, Son of God – chose to adopt the least powerful position in His ministry and, by doing so, the Cause He championed grew in power. This is the invitation God offers to the Anonymous Leader. To become less so that Christ and His Cause can become more. This is the paradox this book invites you to embrace – and, in so doing, gain a front-row seat to watch God do amazing things.

I started writing this book over 12 years ago, long before I ever believed I could actually write a book or offer anything of worth to anyone. But in that time God has taught me lots and now I find myself responding to His promptings to release this work to a wider audience that He might use it to help you lead better. So let's get started – I trust you will enjoy the following chapters and become a better leader because of them.

PART I
THE CONTEXT

1

OF COURSE YOU'RE A LEADER

I CAN STILL recall the moment I first heard the words, 'Of course you're a leader.' Two months beforehand my mother had bought me a ticket to a leadership conference. I was 17 years old and reading *Too Busy Not to Pray* by Bill Hybels at the time, and the book had gripped me, leading me to invite my friends to join me in prayer. My mother was aware of this, and had also discovered Bill Hybels was coming to Melbourne to speak at the conference, and so had booked a ticket for me.

Apart from his book, I didn't know much about the author and so I did some research. I learned Bill Hybels was a pastor of a local church in South Barrington, Illinois, in the US. He had grown the church from no-one to thousands of people. He'd written many books, including the one I had read, which had transformed prayer for me. I was excited and looked forward to my first conference.

At the conference, I hung off every word this captivating speaker said. At the end of the first session, he informed us, 'After the break, we're going to do a test to see who is a leader.' I gulped and turned to my mother, who was sitting next to me. 'I'm not very good at tests, and I'm not sure I'll pass this one.' That was her cue to speak the words that would alter the direction of my life. 'Of course you're a leader.'

As I think back to that exchange, I now realise a few things. First, I think my mother was right. Second, at the time I didn't. Third, I'm glad she was right.

At the time, I would never have called myself a leader, even though those around me would have. They saw something in me that I struggled to see. Every leader has moments of blindness to their own influence. And, of course, a leader doesn't concern themselves with a title – they just lead and people follow. That's what makes them a leader. My mother saw that people wanted to follow me, so she assumed I was a leader.

And people did follow me. I found it easy to convince my friends to meet me at 6 am and pray for people. Not only that but in many cases I also found that people thought my ideas were worth investing in and following. For my part, I couldn't imagine why anyone would say no to coming along – and this, I was to discover, is a key to the leadership gift.

GOD DWELLS IN A LEADER IN SUCH A WAY THAT THE IDEAS THAT DEVELOP AND ARE THEN SHARED HAVE A PERSUASIVE ATTRACTION TO THEM.

What is leadership about?

Leadership is not about the title. It's about the opportunity to lead – and this is an opportunity given by God and entrusted to you by those who follow. That people would dare to follow you is a sobering responsibility.

To follow someone is to invest hope, desires, heart and will in them. It is to surrender their agenda in order to embrace the leader's vision.

As Bill Hybels's second session commenced, I found that the things the speaker shared resonated so deeply within me that I resolved to go and meet him in the lunchbreak. Those near me thought I was crazy but, unperturbed, I walked in the direction I had seen the speaker go. Protecting the door was a huge security guard, so I knew Bill Hybels must be in the room behind the door. I asked the guard if I could have a few moments with the speaker and I was told very clearly, 'No!' I responded by informing the security guard why he should let me pass, telling him the story of my friends and I meeting to pray after reading *Too Busy Not to Pray*.

I think mainly the awkwardness of the moment and the story I told caused the guard to do the only thing he could to shut me up. 'Wait here,' he said. 'I'll be back in a moment.'

He disappeared behind the forbidden doors. What felt like a lifetime passed before he returned. 'Bill has agreed to meet you if you are waiting at the stairs at the foot of the stage two minutes before the next session begins.'

I was ecstatic!

I rushed back to share the news with my mother, although I don't think she believed me. I then moved to the front of the auditorium and, for the next 35 minutes, waited – pen in one hand, book in the other and a stupid expression on my face.

I didn't realise that I shouldn't have done what I did. It never dawned on me that it's not appropriate to hassle security guards and seek the attention of a keynote speaker. And yet, I was the one person that day who had the chance to speak to Bill Hybels, all because I didn't pay attention to the limits others would have seen. For my mother, it was more confirmation that I was a leader.

LEADERS DON'T SETTLE FOR THE STATUS QUO OR REALITY THEY SEE. THEY PURSUE WHAT MOST SAY IS IMPOSSIBLE, WITHOUT ACKNOWLEDGING THIS IS THE CASE. A LEADER REFUSES TO BE LIMITED BY THE THINGS THAT HAVE CREATED LIMITS UP TO THIS POINT. INSTEAD, THEY SEE THE POSSIBILITIES AND INVEST THEMSELVES IN FULFILLING THEM.

The last five minutes of waiting were agony; my heart was racing, palms were sweaty and my throat was dry, and I had just realised I didn't know what I was going to say. Then Bill Hybels appeared. He walked up to me and shook my hand, and I told him how much his book had meant to me and my friends. I told him how God was using what he had written to do amazing work in us and that I was so grateful. He thanked me, signed my book and encouraged me. I floated back to my seat, which I hovered above for the rest of the session – until something even more extraordinary happened.

As the third session gained momentum, Bill Hybels spoke about the early days of his church, Willow Creek Community Church. He told us how God had done a great work and then he said, 'This young guy came up to me in the break. He shared with me how he's been praying and that he then got some friends together, and they've been praying. God is going to use those young people to do amazing things.'

I was 17 years old and had just met the author of a book that had changed my life. I thought meeting the author was significant. But this man understood leadership and knew how to lead. He knew what a leader looked like and, in front of everyone, he affirmed my leadership.

SOMETHING VERY POWERFUL HAPPENS WHEN A SENIOR LEADER ENCOURAGES AN EMERGING LEADER. AUTHORITY AND POWER IS TRANSACTED FROM THE ONE WHO HAS GREAT WEALTH TO THE OTHER WHO IS JUST STARTING OUT.

That moment was formative for me, because of the choice Bill Hybels made to speak courage into my life.

Thankfully, I was too naive and too excited to realise how hard it would actually be.

Leadership is not the goal

Leadership is a gift we are given to use. It should not be an idol we worship, but a catalyst for amazing things to take place. I know people who say, 'I'm not into leadership', as though leadership were something you get into. Leadership is not a noun that you parade around, show off or idolise. It's a verb – an action of service that a person takes to benefit others, not out of choice but out of necessity.

I once interviewed someone for a job. Toward the end of the interview they said, 'I'm kind of over the whole leadership deal. I studied it in college and, to be honest, I don't need to hear another thing about it.' I was looking for a leader, and someone who understands leadership like this isn't a leader.

Leaders don't value what they have learnt until they've discovered whether it works. Leadership is not an academic pursuit of more knowledge. It is an endeavour to help a person or group move forward in the most effective way possible.

Leadership is all about the Cause

I lead because the Cause I serve requires excellence in innovation, creativity and influence, which God has positioned and invited me to offer. Without leadership, a cause is not a cause but an organisation. An organisation does not need movement to be an organisation, but a cause does. And to be moved forward, a cause requires leadership, but the leader, if effective, is not heralded as the hero. Leadership serves the cause, so that the cause can be the hero for the people.

The Cause I have given myself to is the local church. I agree with what Bill Hybels says of the church: 'The local church is the hope of the world.' I am convinced to the core of my being that when Jesus is invited into the centre of someone's life, the fullness of life experienced is incomparable.

I BELIEVE THAT THE CHURCH'S CENTRAL RESPONSIBILITY IS TO ENSURE THAT GOD'S KINGDOM CONTINUES TO ADVANCE IN THIS WORLD. THIS NEEDS TO HAPPEN SO THE LEAST, LOST, LAST AND LONELY FIND THEIR COMPLETE JUSTICE, RESTORATION, HEALTH AND WHOLENESS IN JESUS BY TRUSTING IN GOD. THIS HAS TO BE THE GREATEST CAUSE A PERSON CAN GIVE THEIR LIFE TO.

I have given my life to this Cause and each day I sit in a front-row seat, watching God transform lives. The desire to do this leapt out of me that day when Bill Hybels spoke about leadership. I was already serving and loved the church, but that day my calling clarified and drove me to serve the Cause.

The gift of belief and influencing intentionally

When my mother told me 'Of course you're a leader', I received an invaluable gift. Someone believed in me. My mother saw something within me that I hadn't identified, and helped me see it too.

Naming another's ability to lead is a gift I take every opportunity to offer others. Naming the leadership influence you see in another is not for their benefit. One day it will be, but that should not be your intent. Naming a person's gift for leadership is for the benefit of all those they will lead. If a person can realise they have the ability to intentionally influence others, they can accomplish much for the cause they give themselves to.

We can steward our intentional influence in one of two directions. We can seek to fulfil our self-ambition or we can give ourselves to the cause. The former means we promote ourselves at the cost of everyone and everything. The latter path means we uphold something far greater than we can be and serve its success at the potential expense of ourselves.

In secular leadership, selfish or blind ambition can be understood as necessary to advancing the cause. The result can even be significant achievement, for a time. In Christian leadership, however, the two are mutually exclusive. You cannot pursue your own ambitions without being an obstacle to people seeking to follow Jesus. Perhaps examples in our culture would seem, at first glance, to refute this. Yet spend time in the Biblical narrative, walking in Jesus' footsteps, and you begin to see the tension. The quest, therefore, is to *descend into greatness*, to paraphrase the title of another book by Hybels. Do those leaders who seek the spotlight for themselves help the Cause of Christ? Or do they dissuade people from trusting in Christ? A Christian leader needs to seek to influence people to move toward Jesus and not themselves. Those following don't need a leader invested in power and prestige. They need the cause they are invested in to make a difference for them and in the world. The dilemma is: do we lead toward anonymity or self-ambition?

This dilemma is one every leader encounters. It is a lifelong leadership tension faced every day. Every time a leader gets up to speak. Every time a leader pulls a team together. Every time a leader launches a new initiative, casts a powerful vision, slaves over a complex strategy, meets with a disenchanted follower or chooses to serve the cause behind the scenes. In every circumstance of a leader's engagement, the tension is present: *can I be an Anonymous Leader?* The rest of this book offers ways to help you work with and through this tension, toward anonymity.

DEFINING LEADERSHIP AND ANONYMITY

I STARTED LEADING at the age of 16 (even if I didn't call myself a leader then), and by the age of 19 I had realised how important reading was. I had just taken on the responsibility of leading the youth group I was involved with, and had no idea what I was doing. I wandered into a Christian Bookstore, knowing I needed some help *but* clueless as to where to get it. I said a brief prayer of help, walked around a corner in the store and there it was – literally, the answer to my prayer. I knew the greatest challenge I faced was developing the leaders around me and now, before me on the shelf, sat *Developing the Leaders Around You* by John C. Maxwell.

Since that day I have endeavoured to read like a maniac – as Harry S. Truman said, 'Not all readers are leaders, but all leaders are readers.' I read to increase my skills, learn new things and see the world from a more informed perspective.

Over the years I've read many definitions of leadership. Some authors try to convey the complexity of leadership, while others do the opposite, simplifying it down to a few words. For a long time the simplest definition of leadership I could find was shared by John Maxwell, and belonged to J. Oswald Sanders: 'Leadership is influence.' I like complicated things simplified, so this definition worked for me and I used it.

Leadership gone astray

Knowing what leadership is enables you to identify it in another, and once you identify a leader, you can invite them into leadership. This process worked for me until it started to break down. I kept seeing potential emerging leaders using their influence to disservice people's future through the bad advice they offered. They were not in a position of leadership, but had relational influence. Why people seek advice from those who aren't in a better situation has always puzzled me. Analysing it, I realised these potential leaders were fuelled by personal ambition to influence others. Their goal was to influence a person, rather than to impart wisdom.

This was made clear in the poor advice they would give – advice that would occasionally be dangerous. Further evidence was that the advice they gave to one person would contradict advice they gave to another. Their counsel lacked intentional direction.

The more I talked to people and challenged these emerging influencers, the more I realised my definition of leadership was insufficient. These emerging potential leaders were influencing others but they were not leading them. They were not influencing with a greater vision in mind that would benefit others. I concluded that leadership was not just influence.

Intentional influence

It was several years later when I realised what was missing – leadership was *positive, intentional* influence. I was talking with Lyndal, my wife, explaining that it wasn't enough to equate influence with leadership; instead, it had to be positive and intentional. Positive in that it benefited the person's future completely, separate to what the leader might gain, and intentional in that it assumes direction, vision and focus. I then asked Lyndal what she thought.

At that time Lyndal was producing the Willow Creek Global Leadership Summit. One of her tasks was to familiarise herself with the sessions before they were presented, to choreograph smooth transitions throughout the conference. After hearing my pitch she said, 'You're going to love Joseph Grenny – he defines leadership as intentional influence!' The ideas I had spent years working on were about to be handed to me in two weeks' time. Grenny's talk, titled 'Mastering the Skill of Influence', was excellent. (If you're looking to understand more about influence, I recommend purchasing his book *Influencer*.)

I NOW DEFINE LEADERSHIP AS POSITIVE INTENTIONAL INFLUENCE. THIS MEANS INFLUENCING ANOTHER IN LIGHT OF THE VISION YOU HAVE FOR THEM – A VISION THAT DOES NOT BENEFIT YOURSELF AHEAD OF THE PERSON YOU'RE LEADING. ANYTHING LESS IS EITHER NEGATIVE INFLUENCE OR, WORSE, NEGATIVE INTENTIONAL INFLUENCE.

Is Christian leadership possible?

A little while back I was invited to lead two tutorials in a bachelor-level leadership course. I was excited and enthusiastically engaged in the process. The class participants were eager, even after a long day at work, and we enjoyed high-quality conversation. We explored issues of culture and execution, strategy and change management. The learning for me, however, was in a conversation I had with the course convenor and one of the students, who was also a friend, as we walked to the car park after class.

In the class, we had been discussing the question, 'What is Christian leadership?' Some responses had been offered but none quite satisfied what I felt was a true understanding of Christian leadership.

An opposing phrase

The two terms *Christian* and *leadership* almost seem opposing – even antagonistic. Christianity for many people is a humble, meek, nice religion. It represents a belief system in which people do kind things for others, trying to please everyone and keep the status quo.

Leadership, in many people's minds is quite different. It features a dominant, alpha (usually male) personality ordering his subordinates, and directing them to do exactly as he instructs. So a person could be forgiven for thinking that the term *Christian Leader* is an oxymoron.

As we stood in the car park after class and spoke, it dawned on me. 'Isn't Christian leadership about death?' I asked. Christian leadership moves in the direction of death – of the self. It is always about minimising the self, to become nothing. This stands in contrast to secular leadership, which moves a leader in the direction of becoming something. That's what ambitious leadership is – leading in order to become someone and be proud of what has been created. The more the leader and what they have created can become known, the greater their chance of changing the world. Christian leadership stands in opposition to this.

> **FOR A LEADER TO BE CHRISTIAN, THEY CAN ONLY LEAD A PERSON AS MUCH AS THEY ARE BEING LED BY JESUS CHRIST. CHRISTIAN LEADERS UNDERSTAND IT IS NOT THEM WHO CHANGE THE WORLD. IT IS WHAT GOD DOES THROUGH THEM THAT CHANGES THE WORLD.**

If this is true, for God to do more and more through you, as a Christian leader, something has to make way. That something is you! The goal of the Christian leader is for *the self* to completely die. As this happens, the work and presence of the King are revealed. Christian leadership is at its best when a leader is most transparent.

The secular leader does not need to die to self, because there is nothing to make way for. If they were to begin to die or fade away, they take the cause with them – unless, of course, they are able to pass it on to someone else.

One of the most significant Christian leaders in the early church was the Apostle Paul. He gave his life to the Cause of establishing churches all over the known world. When writing to one of the churches he established at Philippi, he said, 'For to me, to live is Christ and to die is gain.' (Phil 1:21) His sights were set on his Lord and Saviour and the Cause he had been given. If that meant his life would need to be given up for the Cause, he was ready and willing.

Paul was consumed with the spread of the church, as the Gospel took hold of people, but knew it was Jesus who built the church. He wanted to ensure that the positive intentional influence he offered those in the church was on behalf of God – an influence that embodied the positive intentions of God for His people. Paul's life was about becoming so transparent that when people looked at him they saw Jesus. This meant that not only his life but also his death would glorify God.

In his book *Preaching*, Tim Keller says, 'Paul is likening himself to the Holy Spirit, whose job is, like a floodlight, not to point to himself but rather to show us the glory and beauty of Christ. (cf. Jn 16:12-15)' This is precisely what Paul did and what he encourages Anonymous Leaders to do also. The Anonymous Leader uses his influence to point to and highlight the presence of Christ in people's lives, not his own presence.

Whose church is it?

The church belongs to God. Jesus said that He would build His church (Mt 16:18) – which means the church has never been ours to build. The church has been ours to serve, as Christ builds it. Contrary to popular belief, the church's future is not dependent on me developing leaders. Christ develops leaders. My role is to point them toward Christ. When emerging leaders look at seasoned leaders, they need to see Christ building His church. If I can adopt this position, Christ will be able to far more effectively build His church.

CHRISTIAN LEADERSHIP IS THE MOVEMENT OF ONE'S LEADERSHIP AWAY FROM THEMSELVES AND TOWARD CHRIST. THIS INVOLVES OUR DYING TO SELF AND RISING WITH CHRIST.

Having looked at what Christian leadership is, I'd now like to define some of the other terms you will read in this book, which I hope will add to the richness of your reading experience.

Anonymity

Since I can remember I have had a special gift. This gift often reveals itself in social settings when I am meeting people for the first time (or just afterwards). Upon introducing ourselves, we might then have a lengthy conversation. We then part ways – and my special gift kicks in. I have the ability to cause most people who meet me for the first time to forget my name. What's most impressive is that it just happens; I don't even have to strain to get my gift to work.

My gift is most potent in coffee shops. At an airport a few years ago, two friends and I all ordered coffee as we waited to board our plane. The names of the other two guys were called out, followed by a pregnant pause as the girl who served me and now had my coffee in her hand struggled to think of my name. She looked at what she had written. She looked up at me. She looked back at the cup and with deep uncertainty mumbled, 'Coffee for Ruth?' I waited. Surely it had not come to this?

She tried again, more confidently this time, 'Coffee for Ruth!' The two friends I was with began to giggle, uncontrollably. She wound up for her third attempt, which still did not result in a miraculous appearance from Ruth. A crowd had now gathered, and my loyal friends were laughing hysterically as I deeply and very loudly sighed. I walked up and claimed my drink. My gift had struck again.

Unremarkably anonymous

While researching this book, I've reflected on this unremarkable effect I have on strangers. I used to dislike it a lot. I became frustrated that I wasn't important or impressive enough for people to remember my name. As time has passed, my perspective has changed. There is great opportunity in anonymity. When people are not caught up in *me*, I can learn more about them – how they think, what they believe, what they love. In anonymity, my worldview is enriched, my understanding of people deepened and my knowledge of life expanded. Anonymity isn't as bad as I once experienced, but what exactly is it?

The word *anonymity* was created in the late 16th century, derived from the Greek *anōnymos*, which means 'nameless' (from *an-* 'without' and *onym* 'name'). The Oxford dictionary offers two insights:

1. (Of a person) not identified by name; of unknown name.

2. Having no outstanding, individual, or unusual features; unremarkable or impersonal.

The idea of anonymity is that a person be non-identifiable, unreachable or untraceable. Anonymity is about not only being without a name, but also unidentifiable. To be anonymous is to put aside your own identity. In literature when an author wishes to stay anonymous, they adopt a pseudo-identity. This masks their true identity with the false identity of another. Sometimes an author's identity will remain hidden by using the name 'Anonymous'.

Is anonymity a good thing?

Let's address the elephant in the book. Some would argue, and quite rightly, that anonymity is not a good thing – even as we all use the idea of anonymity to protect ourselves. We hide behind 'No Caller ID' options. We avoid the invitation to give our name on feedback forms. We'd prefer our boss simply acted on the information we just gave her anonymously.

Anonymity decreases accountability and increases free expression. Criminals use it to commit a variety of crimes – to acquire personal information from others in the case of identity fraud, for example. Anonymity can be used to allow a person to communicate offensively, or disrespectfully, causing serious repercussions. Unredeemed, anonymity can be used to do great evil.

Anonymity being seen as a bad thing makes sense when we think of people abusing it – hiding behind it, using it to fool and abuse young children, or manipulating it in such a way that financial gain is experienced at the cost of others. However, I believe anonymity has not always been fully appreciated.

Do we want to be anonymous?

Anonymity has another side, which our culture doesn't appreciate. We don't want to be anonymous. We have countless forms of social media and opportunities for self-expression, all of which are to ensure that others know us, or at least part of our lives. We worship pop culture heroes and follow them on Twitter. We buy magazines that have the latest (inaccurate) news on celebrities we idolise, wishing we knew them. Many people feel a deep longing to be famous; to be publically well known.

Wrestling superstar turned actor Dwayne Johnson, aka 'The Rock', recently broke a world record – for the highest number of selfies taken at one time. His record at the time of writing stands at 105 selfies, which Johnson achieved during the launch of his movie *San Andreas*. He crowned himself #selfieking while encouraging a raging narcissistic culture to pursue more of themselves. Anonymity is not something people desire and, for many, it's terrifying. I have a friend whose life goal is to be famous on the internet. Anonymity is not attractive.

If this is the dark side of anonymity, what does redeemed anonymity look like?

THIS SORT OF ANONYMITY IS A TECHNIQUE, OR A WAY OF ENGAGING WITH THE WORLD. THIS ANONYMITY IS ABOUT EMBRACING THE SECURITY OUR IDENTITY OFFERS US, AND SO NOT NEEDING THE ACCLAMATION OR AFFIRMATION OF OTHERS. THIS FREES US TO DO AMAZING THINGS FOR THE CAUSE, WHICH WOULD OTHERWISE NOT BE POSSIBLE.

The awesome side of anonymity

On a Monday evening a friend and I walked from the cinema to my parked car. On the way we passed a bus stop where, under the bench, lay a wallet. I picked it up and searched for some identification, hoping to find a way to reunite the wallet with its owner.

I found an ID, various cards and $15 cash. The ID provided his address and, seeing it was only about a 25-minute drive away, we decided to take the wallet back to him. On the way, a thought entered my mind. When people lose their wallets, their greatest fear is usually that their money, be it via their ATM or credit cards, or simply the physical cash in the wallet, has all been cleaned out. What if this time, instead of that happening, when that young guy opened his returned wallet a couple of hours after losing it, he found more cash in there than he had started with? I loved the idea – it was an exchange of grace – and we had to do it. When we got to the address, an apartment building near the beach, I opened my own wallet and fished out a note and put it in his wallet.

We couldn't get into the building, but we could find the owner's letterbox, so we put the wallet inside. I called the body corporate number on the front door, told them we'd found the wallet and put it in the letterbox, and asked if they could tell the owner it had been delivered. They agreed.

The next day the owner texted me and thanked me for finding his wallet and returning it. He didn't comment on the extra cash or ask why I would bring the wallet back at all. I like to think he was left wondering about how the extra money came to be in his wallet and why a complete stranger would return anything to him. With no person to thank, his thoughts of gratitude and appreciation may just have been offered to God – the orchestrator of all things.

This is a small example of what redeemed anonymity is, which holds greater power when leading someone.

ANONYMITY HAS THE POTENTIAL TO DO MUCH EVIL, BUT REDEEMED ANONYMITY HAS GREAT POWER TO DO MUCH GOOD.

The creator revealed

In the study of historical art pieces, occasionally a piece of art is found that doesn't carry the insignia of the artist. An expert art curator is not worried by this. They are able to identify who the artist is likely to be by close examination of the particular characteristics and style of the piece. Identifying factors include the composition of the colours, use of materials, style of stroke and shape of form. All these clues point toward the true identity of the artist. The task of Anonymous Leaders is to ensure that the clues we leave behind point to Christ. The flavour of our leadership originates with us, but needs to leave the identifying evidence of Christ in our wake.

In 2012 *Embracing Obscurity* was published, authored by 'Anonymous'. It was a stroke of genius to credit this book's authorship to that name. As I read the book's reviews, a tension began to emerge. At first, people seemed to be less inclined to give the book much credit because they didn't know who the author was. Then things began to shift. People started to give the book more credit than if they had known the author. Readers were forced to wrestle with the black and white of what was written, which was confronting to them.

The author's words seemed to increase in authority, as people realised they were now wrestling with what God was saying to them through the pages. Previously they could have discredited the work because they had discredited something about the author. I don't know if the author had this effect in mind when he or she wrote the book, but it does reveal the power anonymity can have if redeemed for good.

To become anonymous is to become hidden in Christ

As an Anonymous Leader, your goal is to become hidden in Christ – transparent so that Christ can be seen in your life. Paul epitomised this. When he wrote to the church he planted in Corinth he said, 'Follow my example, as I follow the example of Christ.' (1 Cor 11:1) And later, 'Therefore I urge you to imitate me.' (1 Cor 4:16) To be hidden in Christ is not to be hidden altogether, but to represent Christ so significantly that you become synonymous with him.

Paul said, 'if you have been raised with Christ, seek the things that are above, where Christ is, seated at the right hand of God. Set your minds on things that are above, not on things that are on earth, for you have died, and your life is hidden with Christ in God.' (Col 3:1–3) Paul gives us a clue as to how we might begin to achieve this impossible task.

Paul instructs us, in light of our new identity, to seek things that are above. The word 'seek' is written in the present imperative, which means it is continuous and ongoing. That is, 'if you have been raised with Christ', constantly and for as long as it takes 'seek the things that are above, where Christ is'. This phrase isn't a 21st-century cultural reference to heaven, but a reference to the sovereign reign of God. God's sovereignty is about how we understand God's power, character, presence and joy, as God interacts with us. Paul urges us to continually set our mind to these things. We are presented with a choice to concentrate on the sovereignty of God, or on earthly things such as honour, position and advancement; the things we are ambitious to secure.

The antidote to the distracting power of ambition

Ambition has great power to distract a leader charged with furthering the Cause of Christ. Paul knows the power of ambition and the threat it poses to our leadership for Christ, so he calls us to concentrate on the Cause to which we have been called. This requires that we turn from our ambition toward Christ.

It doesn't feel natural to deny the ambitions we have and, without Christ, denying them is impossible. The antidote to ambitions' allure is a vibrant relationship with Christ. The more time we spend with Christ, the more He imparts His heart to us. Ambition is not something we have to beat. It has already been beaten by Christ. We have the fruit of Christ's victory, which is far greater than ambitions' prize. When we hide away with Christ, on a daily basis, it becomes easier to hide from ambition. I'll address more of this in chapter 14.

The Cause

'Give me a cause worth dying for!' We were sitting in a staff meeting talking about vision when Mike, one of my colleagues, put forward this sentiment. Vision makes all people thrive, even when it's not recognised as vision. Every time a political election is held, policies are advertised that offer us a better future. When we interview for a job we hope we'll get it, so our future will be improved. When we think about dating, falling in love, marrying, having kids, buying a house and even retiring – those thoughts and decisions are all about vision.

What is the best picture of my future that I would like to see become a reality? That is the question we all are constantly asking.

Belonging to a future

A cause incorporates an opportunity to belong to something that creates a better future for people. It moves and grows and advances, and sweeps us up along the way. It connects with our core values, excites us and changes us. A cause is:

1. a person or thing that gives rise to an action, phenomenon or condition

2. a principle, aim or movement to which one is committed and which one is prepared to defend or advocate

3. (as a verb) to make something happen.

A CAUSE EMBODIES STRONG VALUES THAT COMPEL PEOPLE TO JOIN IN, TO MOVE IN THE SAME DIRECTION, TO SEE CHANGE TAKE PLACE. 'GIVE ME A CAUSE WORTH DYING FOR' IS THE CRY OF THE HUMAN HEART.

It was the same for the disciples. Before meeting Jesus they lived oppressed by a cause that the Romans held dear: world domination. They were the Jews who were dominated by the force of nature that was the Roman Empire – that is, until that life-changing conversation they each had with Jesus, when He invited them into His Cause. His Cause would see them transformed by the grace of God and empowered by the Holy Spirit to action God's plans and desires for the world.

The Cause is the Kingdom

As soon as Jesus was baptised He was driven by the Spirit into the desert to face temptation, which strengthened His resolve. We then read, 'From that time on Jesus began to preach, "Repent, for the Kingdom of Heaven has come near."' (Mt 4:17) What we call the Cause of Christ, Christ calls the approaching and current reality of his Kingdom. In *The Divine Conspiracy*, Dallas Willard says of Jesus' Cause, 'This is a call for us to reconsider how we have been approaching our life, in light of the fact that we now, in the presence of Jesus, have the option of living within the surrounding movements of God's eternal purposes, of taking our life into his.'

Jesus' words force us to reconsider our own lives. The presentation of a worthy cause does that. Jesus presents us with the option to live within the surrounding movements of what God has begun now and will continue on throughout eternity. A cause is the opportunity to be part of something greater than us, which is not about us. This is what Jesus welcomes His disciples into – a movement that will usher in a new vision, one that every human soul longs for.

THE ANONYMOUS LEADER IS THE ONE WHO TAKES UP THIS CAUSE AS HIS OWN. HE CHAMPIONS IT AMONG PEERS AND FOLLOWERS, AND THOSE WHOM HE POSITIVELY AND INTENTIONALLY INFLUENCES.

When asked by His disciples how they should pray, Jesus led them with these words, 'Your Kingdom come, Your will be done, on earth as it is in heaven.'(Mt 6:10) For Jesus, the Cause was seeing the reality of heaven invade earth. The Kingdom of Heaven or Kingdom of God, as Jesus would have understood it, was the full expression of God's reality.

In God's Kingdom, where God reigns, sin does not. People often think of heaven as a place where pain ceases and peace abounds, but the Kingdom of Heaven is more than this. When the Kingdom of God invades this world, all balance, health and wholeness is restored, as those struggling to find themselves without God are reclaimed by grace. Wrongdoing, injustice and hatred are redeemed and transformed into righteousness, justice and love. This is the Kingdom of God and the ultimate Cause Christ came to usher in.

When Jesus prayed those words, He was revealing (to those who could grasp it), that the realities of His Father's Kingdom could be seen now. So Jesus urges His followers to pray that God's reality will become our reality. Jesus' desire is that the essence of God's Kingdom will become the essence of our experience in this world. He taught His disciples to pray this, as He would have prayed this – a prayer that mysteriously catalysed the arrival of Jesus' Kingdom.

Acting as a signpost for the Cause

Transformation in a person's life only happens when God's Kingdom affects our reality. John the Baptist was aware of this and the role his leadership needed to play. His role was to compel people to see the Kingdom, to be a signpost that pointed others toward it. The thing about a signpost is that people forget it when they reach their destination – in this case, experiencing the freedom the Kingdom of God offers them.

THE CAUSE OF CHRIST IS TO FULFIL THE WILL OF GOD. GOD'S WILL IS WHAT GOD DETERMINES TO HAPPEN. IT IS GOD'S GREATEST PLEASURE OR DESIRE. OUT OF THE INFINITE CHOICES GOD HAS, HIS WILL IS WHAT HE MOST WANTS TO HAPPEN.

We see through Jesus' life that God wills His Kingdom to come to earth. God wills that the wonders and glories of heaven are not something we are on a waiting list for when we die. They can be our reality now. In Jesus' first moments of ministry, His Father's Kingdom began to advance, developing into a movement called the church.

The place of leadership in the Cause

When I heard Scot McKnight speak in Chicago in 2014, he said, 'What Jesus called the Kingdom, Paul called the church. They are identical but not the same.' The church is the Kingdom of God with flesh on it. We are the church. What makes us the church is the Spirit of God dwelling in us; individually and corporately.

For the church to move forward, empowered by the Holy Spirit, God has called leaders; diligent leaders who God has gifted to lead. To lead effectively these gifted leaders must be filled with the Holy Spirit.

Defining leadership and anonymity

Just before He ascended to heaven, Jesus told His disciples – the future leaders of the church – that they would receive power when the Holy Spirit came on them. Then they would be Jesus' witnesses in Jerusalem, and in all Judea and Samaria, and to the ends of the earth. (Acts 1:8) A witness is someone who declares, to those who are yet to see, something they have already seen. The disciples received the Holy Spirit, became witnesses to the goodness and grace of God and were empowered to tell everyone about it. When leaders start to share what they have witnessed, people are influenced toward it.

More people came to faith and the Church grew, but it wasn't long before they faced some issues. Two major ones were feeding the poor and looking after the widows. 'So the Twelve gathered all the disciples together and said, "It would not be right for us to neglect the ministry of the word of God in order to wait on tables. Brothers and sisters, choose seven men from among you who are known to be full of the Spirit and wisdom. We will turn this responsibility over to them and will give our attention to prayer and the ministry of the word."' (Acts 6:2–4)

It was essential that a task such as this was stewarded by leaders who were full of the Holy Spirit, because it is Christ's Cause. A group of people only becomes the church when they know Christ and are inhabited by the Holy Spirit. To lead this group of people forward requires a leader who is in a vibrant relationship with Christ and is in tune with that same Spirit who breathed the gathering into being.

If the Church is a gathering of people who are defined by the presence of the Holy Spirit – dwelling among them and directing their movements – then every leader in the Church must also be filled with the Holy Spirit. This is a central aspect of Anonymous Leadership. Only a leader who is filled with the Holy Spirit can become anonymous. A leader often has a deep desire to take something which is not what it could be and turn it into something amazing. Accompanying this desire is the need to be recognised for their efforts.

WITHOUT THE PRESENCE OF GOD LIVING IN A LEADER, NOTHING ABSORBS THE RECOGNITION GIVEN.

This means that, without God at work in us, we will take the credit instead of God. Taking the credit is not a bad thing, but it does feed our ambition and lead us away from recognising what God has done in and through us.

Only by the Holy Spirit dwelling in a leader – defining, encouraging, shaping, holding, chastising and challenging them – can true anonymity be attained. Without the power of the Holy Spirit alive in us, we are unable to free ourselves from the ambitious quest our hearts long for. Only by the Spirit of God living in us can we fully develop wisdom, integrity, resilience, humility and security.

The Anonymous Leader does not seek recognition. Paul said to the Galatians, 'Am I now trying to win the approval of human beings, or of God? Or am I trying to please people? If I were still trying to please people, I would not be a servant of Christ.'(Gal 1:10) To please people is to chase ambition and, as Paul says, this prevents us from being a servant of Christ.

WHEN RECOGNITION COMES, THE ANONYMOUS LEADER REALISES THE PRAISE RECEIVED BELONGS TO THE ONE WHO DEFINES AND LIVES WITHIN HER. JUST AS WHEN THE VOID OF RECOGNITION AND APPRECIATION RAGES, THE ANONYMOUS LEADER DOESN'T GO IN SEARCH OF IT. INSTEAD, SHE GIVES IN AND LISTENS TO GOD'S QUIET VOICE OF APPRECIATION AND AFFIRMATION.

This is what it means to lead forward the Cause of Christ, such that the Cause's true Leader is seen and recognised as we point others toward Him.

Ambition

This is embarrassing to admit, but for a long time it was my ambition to lead a large church. My peers at Theological College suspected I one day would. The particular denomination I belong to, the Uniting Church, doesn't have many large churches, and coming out of College I didn't know any. (I realise this is a gross way of thinking about it, but bear with me.)

I was equally keen to minister wherever God would place me, and do so with the understanding I would grow a church. I never publicly declared my aspirations to lead a large church but did share them with close friends in moments of vulnerability. I thought this was an admirable goal – but my intentions were misplaced.

GOD NEVER WANTED ME TO AMBITIOUSLY PURSUE THE NEED FOR MORE INFLUENCE WITH MORE PEOPLE. GOD DOESN'T EVEN NEED ME TO BUILD HIS CHURCH.

God created the universe, so building a church can't be too much of a strain on Him. It did take God awhile to get through to me, though.

The false allure of greatness

I remember the place I was when everything changed for me. I was ministering at Seymour Uniting Church in central Victoria, where I had been for four years. In that time we had seen the church parish grow from 75 regular attenders to 160 regulars. It was a wonderful season of ministry, and I still value it deeply. People put their faith in Christ, transformed by the power of the Gospel, and we reached into our community with grace and service. It was exciting and fulfilling and I loved the people.

Then I received a phone call – and an invitation to investigate a potential call to minister in one of the largest churches in Victoria. I'd heard little about this church, but I felt a deep honour and great excitement that they had sought me out. *Wow*, I thought, *my dream is coming true*. I went into the conversation with a strange mixture of excitement and trepidation. I had no desire to leave Seymour – it was our home where our friends were and we loved the church – but it was an amazing opportunity, which I had to explore.

Lyndal and I drove to the church and met with the relevant people, who were wonderful. We had a great time and discussed the exciting opportunities. The only real question that matters in this sort of conversations is, 'Was this the place God was calling us to?' When making a decision of this magnitude, this question supersedes all others.

It was a large, successful church. Our theologies and philosophy of ministry and leadership seemed to be a good match. I needed to look at what I felt I was prepared for, and we needed to find clarity on a few minor complications, but it was looking promising. Our conversation concluded with a tour of the church.

We stepped into the huge room and I gawked around me. 'Oh, to preach to this many people,' a dark inner voice whispered. I wandered throughout the seats and up on to the platform. I started to feel a sense of unease and I couldn't shrug it off. Was this to be the next chapter for me?

On the platform was a huge communion table, sitting right on the front edge of the stage. I walked up to one side of it and gently attempted to lift it, testing if it was bolted to the floor or could be moved. As I did so, our guide said, 'If you're thinking about moving that table, think again. The table stays front and centre. You'll have an uprising on your hands if you try to move it.'

Large churches have problems as much as small churches, but the problems get bigger and more complex the larger a church grows. I hadn't realised this up until this moment. I had been pursuing an ambitious dream, convinced it would be easy to pastor a large church.

As those words came out of our guide's mouth, my ambitious dream shattered – and I gained some significant insights about myself. My ambition to lead a large church was rooted in what it would communicate to those who knew me. People would think I had 'made it' – I would think I had 'made it' – and I had been entertaining this ambitious goal that clouded my awareness of what God was calling me to do.

As the pieces of my ambitious dream fell apart around me, I clearly saw where God was calling me. It wasn't to this church, even though the challenge of the communion table excited me. He was calling me to stay in Seymour.

I didn't want issues that weren't mine. I wanted issues that God was calling me to face, and this opportunity was not what God was calling me to. I realised that my greatest desire was to do what God wanted me to do. To do it in the place where God wanted me to do it, for as long as God required me to do it.

That day God put to death my ambitions to be seen as a successful leader who had 'made it'. Leading a large church is an admirable task, best suited to an Anonymous Leader, which one day I might be honoured enough to do. If that day comes, I will only be able to lead the church with excellence if God has first ensured the anonymity of my leadership.

I let the people I'd met with know I felt God wasn't calling me to that place, and had renewed my call to Seymour. It was the truth.

Ironically, as I write this book I am on the ministry team at Newlife, one of the larger churches in the Uniting Church in Australia. The process to come here was long and drawn out; my prerogative. I battled with God, trying to convince him that I wasn't called to lead in a large church. I did all I could to escape the call, and stay in the safe confines of what I knew in Seymour. As I shared before, my greatest desire isn't tied to any type of church. My greatest desire is to do exactly what God wants me to do, in exactly the place where God wants me to do it, for as long as God requires me to do it. It just so happens that what God was calling me to was to serve at Newlife, a larger church. But I did and do attempt to lead here with a spirit of anonymity.

God used what had happened in previous church-calling conversations to prepare my soul for what He was orchestrating. God needed the pride and ambition in me to shrivel up. Only then could I surrender completely to His call, and not be distracted by my ambitions, which would have disabled my ministry.

Ambition in the Bible

The New Testament uses the word *ambition* seven times. Each time it has several commonalities. Never is it a desirable trait, and is only featured in words of warning from Biblical writers. In the Bible, ambition is always connected to the idea of selfish gain – to be all about self-promotion.

Two such examples are when Paul says, 'Do nothing from selfish ambition or conceit, but in humility regard others as better than yourselves.' (Phil 2:3) And when James, thought to be the brother of Jesus, writes, 'For where there is envy and selfish ambition, there will also be disorder and wickedness of every kind.' (Jas 3:16) The Greek word for ambition, *eritheia*, was widely used in the first century. It referred to a person who was electioneering or investigating the potential to fill a public office. The political scene was rife with men who found their place in public office but did nothing to serve the public, instead using their positions as a stage for self-promotion and indulgences. Christian leaders responded to this with great disdain and so the word came to be used in the manner we see Paul and James write – ambitiously pursuing greater influence at the cost of those meant to be served.

TO BE AMBITIOUS WAS TO PUT ONE'S SELF FORWARD TO ENSURE PERSONAL GAIN AT THE COST OF OTHERS WHO WERE NOT ELECTED. AMBITIONS LEAD TO A FRACTIOUS SPIRIT, CONSUMING A LEADER WITH IDEAS OF SELF-GAIN.

It is this understanding of ambition I want to respond to in the chapters that follow. This selfish or blind ambition lurks in the heart of every leader and, if left unchecked, can dismantle our influence right before our eyes. Yet if acknowledged, understood and redeemed, we can find ourselves heading toward the wonderful intrigue and mystery of Anonymous Leadership.

Redeemed ambition

You may be wondering why I've been so harsh on ambition. Am I saying it's bad to be ambitious? If we're using the definition of ambition I've just outlined, then, yes, it's an undesirable attribute for a Christian leader.

What then do we do with Paul's writing to the Philippians, 'I want to know Christ – yes, to know the power of his resurrection and participation in his sufferings, becoming like him in his death'? (Phil 3:10) That sounds ambitious. So perhaps we need another word that allows for redeemed ambition without the confusion. I suggest we use the word *driven* in the place of ambitious. We need to be driven so the causes we give ourselves to can flourish.

Another example is found in Paul's farewell to the Ephesians when he says, 'However, I consider my life worth nothing to me; my only aim is to finish the race and complete the task the Lord Jesus has given me – the task of testifying to the good news of God's grace.' (Acts 20:24) Paul seems very ambitious here, but I would counter that he was not ambitious as much as he was determined. He was determined to achieve a task he had been given. In achieving it he would benefit others, whom he was serving.

In Scripture, negative connotations cling to ambition, whereas the ideas behind *driven* and *determined* redeem ambition. They achieve the same purpose but maintain a sense of servanthood. If we use the Biblical meaning for ambition – selfish ambition – we are then permitted to more clearly see the power of anonymity.

3

LEARNING FROM JOHN THE BAPTIST

Missing out on the credit

Leadership is tough. A leader pours countless hours into countless lives, with the hope that God transforms and then uses those lives. I worked with one young person who, over the time I knew him, was transformed by Christ. The integral part I played in his journey was a privilege.

When the time came for him to move to another city, we threw a party for him, during which his father asked to say a few words. His dad shared the impact he had seen God make on his son's life. It was an emotional moment. The father paused and then thanked the leader who he felt had been significant in his son's formation. I was shocked to hear I was not the leader he identified.

The father continued to celebrate the impact this leader, one of my friends, had had on his son, enabling him to stay in the faith and church. Thanking him profusely, he concluded his speech. That was all great, but

I felt that speech belonged to me. I was the one who was meant to be highlighted and celebrated. It was me who had done much of the work.

I was disappointed – at first with the speech but then in my reaction to it. I was annoyed that I had felt the need to be acknowledged – as Carl Lentz, Pastor of Hillsong Church New York, said, 'I don't get disappointed any more when I don't get recognition. I now get disappointed if I need it.' I was in that tension.

A leader constantly faces this situation. Where the ambitious leader struggles when they are not recognised, however, the Anonymous Leader views it as an unentitled blessing. They are more concerned with the carrying out of God's will than with the thanks they will get from doing it. A powerful illustration of this is found in the New Testament after 400 years of God's silence.

The Kingdom of Heaven is near

He was a wild man – thought by some to be crazy, by others strange, and to the rest fanatical. He came to usher in a new regime. Bending steadfast traditions to create new understandings, he was an innovator. He was unlike anyone who had been seen before. Some called him a prophet. Others would call him the Messiah. Was he a genius willing to risk everything on a hunch?

His name was John, and he lived in the desert. Comfort was of no interest to him nor was popularity, fame or fortune. Those who met him said he ate wild honey and feasted on the locusts he caught. His clothing came from the land, woven together from camel hair, pulled together with a leather belt.

He was a risk taker, an innovator; his influence was substantial, and the wisdom he offered attractive. In fact, people came from as far as Jerusalem and the entire Jordan region to find this mad man on the outskirts of Judea.

'Repent, for the Kingdom of Heaven has come near' captures what John was about. To John, repentance meant a change of allegiance and priorities. John was urging people to evaluate what they were devoted to. He urged them to look at whom they were following and what they were trusting in – and for John and what was about to happen, this was an issue of immediacy.

The Kingdom of Heaven was closer than it had ever been. God's Kingdom was nearly upon them, and John longed for the people to see this. If they could see and experience this Kingdom, society could find its complete redemption.

'Repent, for the Kingdom of Heaven has come near' became synonymous with John's ministry. The words of a loving leader consumed by an outrageous idea, for which he was willing to risk everything in order to make it known. John was the original Anonymous Leader. His thoughts were not chained to how he looked, what others perceived him to be about, or the thousands of years of culture he was challenging. His thoughts led him into action. That action was not about being countercultural, although he was. He wasn't reacting to something in his culture. No. He was offering something new that people needed and that, if accepted, could redeem culture.

He was a leader. He was John the Baptist.

The Baptist

They called him the Baptist not because his parents had given him an awkward and strange middle and last name but because this title defined what he did. John baptised people in the Jordan River. He accompanied them into the water, heard their confession and then immersed them. It was a new day and a new way of doing things. For this to make sense, we must realise that baptism was not a foreign concept.

The Jewish people had been facilitating baptism for years as one of a number of entry rituals Gentiles would undertake to become Jews. To be baptised, the person would enter the water alone, submerge themselves and then exit, to be greeted by the community witnessing the event.

John was different.

The prophet Isaiah had spoken of him, saying he was 'A voice of one calling in the wilderness "Prepare the way for the Lord; make straight paths for him."' (Mk 1:3) John embraced this announcement with one of his own. He baptised Jews and Gentiles into this new reality to signify something even greater than the Jewish leaders were willing to affirm; the Messiah was close.

Using environments to point to the Cause

When I teach or explore this passage, I always ask people, 'Did you take note of the location where John was baptising people?' I do so because the location John chose was strategic, and not accidental.

THE ANONYMOUS LEADER'S PRIMARY ROLE IS TO CREATE ENVIRONMENTS IN WHICH TRANSFORMATION CAN TAKE PLACE. WHEN ENVIRONMENTAL FACTORS BECOME THE CATALYST FOR GOD TO TRANSFORM A PERSON, PEOPLE ARE MOVED TOWARD THE CAUSE AND NOT THE LEADER.

This is why John chooses the Jordan River. As far as rivers go, the Jordan was handy because it was close. Other than that, it was the same as other rivers – with one exception. The Jordan River was an anchor point of faith for many of those coming to John to be baptised.

The Jordan marked the end of a 40-year trek through the desert for the Jewish people. In the book of Exodus we read how Moses, trusting God, led the people through the desert to the Promised Land. The Jordan marked the final obstacle between them and what God had promised.

Moses was an Anonymous Leader. We see it in his leadership, especially in the 31st chapter of Deuteronomy. 'I am now a hundred and twenty years old and I am no longer able to lead you. The Lord has said to me, "You shall not cross the Jordan." The Lord your God Himself will cross over ahead of you.' Years earlier, Moses had lost the right to lead the people through the Jordan (see chapter 10 for more on this). What I love is, in spite of that, we don't see a trace of bitterness or regret in Moses. He is still in awe that God would use him and grateful for the opportunity to worship God. Moses concludes his leadership with the Promised Land in sight and says, 'The Lord himself will go ahead of you.'

Moses helps us see that he was not the true leader. God was, and even in Moses' permanent absence, God will continue in God's faithfulness. It was God who first had the idea to free His people and invited Moses to adopt the Cause. Moses obliged and walked each step in loving service of God and the people.

Moses dies and Joshua steps into leadership – also called by God to lead the people. He rallies them on the banks of the Jordan, consecrates them and focuses them, and they follow him. First the priests take a step of faith into the water, and this is then copied by each of the Israelites behind them. They step into the flooded waters of the Jordan and God does something miraculous in the river. Somewhere upstream, the Jordan stops flowing. So the people complete the crossing on dry ground.

For a Jew, the Jordan was about coming home. It was about transitioning from lost desert wanderings to owning and residing in secure land, from poverty to prosperity, from being lost to being found, moving away from slavery and oppression and into freedom and liberation.

The Jordan held such powerful meanings for all Israelites, and John recreated this as a spiritual reality through baptism, giving them a similar experience to what their forefathers had. He uses the environment to enable people to connect with the Cause and join it. John hoped that when people reflected back on their baptism they did not remember who baptised them, but rather what they were baptised into. A new Kingdom whose king, Jesus, loved them, because the baptism was what prepared them for the ministry of Jesus.

THIS IS WHAT AN ANONYMOUS LEADER DOES. HE CREATES ENVIRONMENTS THAT HELP PEOPLE BUY INTO THE CAUSE. WHEN THIS IS EFFECTIVE, THE ANONYMOUS LEADER DOESN'T CARE IF HE IS REMEMBERED.

The voice that announces the Cause

John was the voice that Isaiah had foretold: a lone voice leading people into a new reality. A reality that was far greater than John – his role was to open the door for those wanting to enter. This was his message: 'After me comes the one more powerful than I, the straps of whose sandals I am not worthy to stoop down and untie.' (Mk 1:7)

These were John's words of preparation as he spoke of Jesus. John positioned himself to be the announcer of Jesus. His entire leadership contribution is only validated when the one whom he announces shows up. Without Jesus' arrival, without the Kingdom of Heaven coming to bear, John was just a crazy wild man running around the desert, eating insects. John staked his leadership on the authenticity of the Cause, and wasn't interested in personal or selfish ambition. He was only interested in Jesus' arrival on the scene. Jesus was the long-awaited Saviour: God with us and among us. The Messiah who John was convinced he was not worthy to even serve.

Worthy of the King

Servants in the first century were aplenty. One of their roles was to untie a visitor's sandals as he or she stepped over the threshold of a home. This act required the servant to humble themselves at the feet of the guest. John takes this metaphor, saying he is not worthy to even untie Jesus' sandals.

John and Jesus were cousins, related by blood. Their mothers shared the joy of pregnancy together. So what John says is astounding.

John knew Jesus was the one everyone had been waiting for. He declares to all who would listen that his cousin, Jesus, is about to usher in something truly incomprehensible, and John knew that to serve a man who is to do this is an honour beyond imagination. John's entire approach is grounded in humility. And this is all from a man who spoke of his childhood friend. The closer John grew to Jesus the man, the more he revered His divinity.

'Then Jesus came from Galilee to the Jordan to be baptised.' (Mt 3:13) That small word, *then*, causes us to realise the essence of John's purpose.

We aren't told how long John had been baptising people – it doesn't matter. John's heart was to serve his Lord by ensuring he played his part – to announce the coming Messiah. To John, time was inconsequential. It is also like this for the Anonymous Leader who, regardless of the effort, cost or struggle, will hold to her calling to serve the Cause for as long as it takes.

FOR THE ANONYMOUS LEADER, QUITTING IS NOT AN OPTION. A DEEP RESILIENCE GRIPS TIGHT, WITH WHITE-KNUCKLED DETERMINATION, TO ENSURE THAT THE CAUSE BEING USHERED IN IS ENCOUNTERED.

John was a resilient leader.

Jesus' desire to be baptised affronted John, who says, 'I need to be baptised by you, and you come to me?' Jesus responds with, 'Let it be so now; it is proper for us to do this to fulfil all righteousness.' (Mt 3:15) With intention, Jesus spoke John's language – John was all about fulfilling righteousness – and so he consented. They waded into the Jordan and John the Baptist baptised Jesus. It was a powerful moment as God spoke and Jesus was filled with the Holy Spirit, signifying the beginning of Jesus' ministry.

Once Jesus was baptised, John retired and moved back home, where he lived a content life knowing that he had fulfilled his calling. Well, not quite.

Of all the options available to John after baptising Jesus, retirement was the one he never would have taken. Retirement is a western cultural ideal anyway – the Bible only has one form of retirement, and it's called death. Things did change for John, but they also did not change. In fact, we see his resolve to lead anonymously only intensify.

What next?

John had reinvented ceremonial washing. In a few short years, it was adopted by the early church as a ritual – an outward sign of an inward change. It became a public declaration of a changed and re-sworn allegiance to Christ. Of course, this was going to create some conflict.

After being baptised, Jesus left John, but a short time later they were reunited at Aenon near Salim. Jesus began baptising people in the water, and while doing so an argument broke out between John's disciples and a certain Jew.

This argument has John's disciples asking him, 'Rabbi, that man who was with you on the other side of the Jordan – the one you testified about – look, he is baptising, and everyone is going to him.' (Jn 3:26)

John's response is simple: 'A person can receive only what is given them from heaven.' John understood that everything he had was a gift from heaven. The purpose to which he had been called was a gift he was thankful for. This is the platform that the Anonymous Leader stands upon, which we will explore in the next chapters. His disciples didn't understand. No-one could understand why John felt it was an honour to stand in the shadow of the Messiah. (Jn 3)

Highlighted here are the two types of leadership this book examines.

THERE ARE LEADERS WHO LEAD FOR PERSONAL AMBITION, IN ORDER TO BE KNOWN, TO BE CELEBRATED AND TO BE REMEMBERED. THE ANONYMOUS LEADER DOES NOT CARE FOR THESE THINGS. INSTEAD, THEY HAVE GIVEN THEIR LIVES, REPUTATION AND LEGACY TO THE CAUSE THEY LEAD, IN ORDER THAT IT WILL MAKE A DIFFERENCE IN PEOPLE'S LIVES.

Why be remembered?

Ricardo Semler in his TED Talk 'How to Run a Company with (Almost) No Rules' asks the question, 'Why do I want to be remembered at all?' He goes on to reveal that this question took him different places. The Anonymous Leader is interested in those different places. It is in those different places that we become part of something far greater than ourselves.

John the Baptist dealt with this question in the years before he ever faced the baptised Messiah. Everything about John reflected that he understood who he was as a leader, and who he wasn't. As Anonymous Leaders we must strive to understand ourselves in the same way.

Finding your place

John knew his place and purpose and was secure in it. He tells us, 'I am not the Messiah but am sent ahead of him.'(Jn 3:28) He didn't need a pat on the back from Jesus or from God. He didn't need the crowds chanting his name, or keeping score of how many baptisms he'd done. He found his assurance in what he had been asked to do. He was completely secure in what God had invited him to do, because of who had invited him, not what he had been asked to do.

Being caught up in wanting to be as influential as others are is easy. The road to anonymity, however, allows you to let all of that go and cling to the calling of God.

THE ANONYMOUS LEADER KNOWS THAT THE MEASURE OF HER INFLUENCE IS BIRTHED OUT OF HER FAITHFULNESS TO WHAT GOD HAS ASKED HER TO DO. SHE DOESN'T TRY TO MANUFACTURE MORE INFLUENCE OR MORE FOLLOWERS. THE ANONYMOUS LEADER FINDS CONTENTMENT AND THEN FREEDOM IN JUST DOING WHAT SHE HAS BEEN ASKED BY GOD TO DO.

This freedom defined John's life, and is expressed best in one grand statement (which ironically ensured he was remembered for all of time): 'He must become greater; I must become less.' (Jn 3:30)

In eight words John summarises everything about his life, and these words are the catchcry of the Anonymous Leader. John reveals to all that he is a friend to Jesus and not his competitor. This revelation is what leads those still weighing up their options to give their allegiance to Christ.

Can you imagine John's disciples listening to this? Maybe it was the first time they had heard their leader say it. We don't know how many disciples John had, but we do know they followed him. In their eyes, John was the one most worthy of their followership – they had pledged their allegiance and committed their lives to him. He was the one in whose shadow they chose to dwell. How challenging it must have been for them to hear their leader say, 'He must become greater; I must become less.'

If John were to become less what would that mean for them?

Their leader, who was supposed to be growing in fame and notoriety, was now retreating from the spotlight, which would affect their identity as well as John's.

They would have immediately assessed their motives. Suddenly their intentions were exposed. They either committed to the Cause John was aligned with and, in doing so, signed away their own ambition, or they found another Rabbi to follow.

Might John's words reveal the true yearnings of our own hearts?

What motivates you?

What would you think if your leader said, 'If all goes well with the church we're ministering in or the cause we're championing or the ministry we're growing, when we reach our goals, we'll all not only be out of a job but we also won't be asked to lead anything by anyone whom we influence or who hears about what we've done'?

Would you still follow?

Would you still put your life and heart on the line and commit with all your enthusiasm and passion to the cause? It's a confronting question that reveals the personal ambition that lurks in our hearts.

IF WE DON'T DILIGENTLY UPROOT OUR AMBITION, WE WILL NEVER BE ABLE TO GIVE EVERYTHING TO WHAT GOD ASKS US TO. A FAILURE TO ADDRESS THE AMBITION WITHIN US MEANS WE WILL ALWAYS KEEP SOMETHING SAVED UP OR SET ASIDE TO BENEFIT US.

It's all about the Cause

John's wanderings weren't isolated to the desert. He liked to challenge the political elite of the day, and so it wasn't long before he found himself in prison under the guard of Herod's soldiers. He had allegedly told King Herod that he should not claim Herodias, his brother Philip's wife, for his pleasure. This infuriated Herod, leading to John's arrest. John, considered to be a prophet, saw it as his duty to challenge the integrity of the king if he was to venture into immoral territory.

John would have met his demise sooner, but Herod was fearful of the people rioting if John was executed. As John sat in prison, Jesus continued His ministry, healing the sick, giving sight to the blind, restoring the lame. Word of His influence spread and made its way to John, who did something that has created much conjecture ever since.

Upon hearing what Jesus was doing, John sent word to his disciples, telling them to find Jesus and ask, 'Are you the one who is to come, or are we to wait for another?' (Lk 7:18)

It is unclear why John would ask this and what he is actually asking. Was he feeling insecure and defeated in prison awaiting his death, and so wanted to check that he'd not wasted his life? Was it actually a way of affirming Jesus' ministry and ensuring that what he was hearing was the truth? Did he in fact want his disciples to realise that Jesus was the Messiah and he was not?

Wherever you land on these questions, one thing remains clear. John the Baptist, up until his final breath, was more concerned about the success and reign of the Messiah than he was about his own predicament. Of all the things he could have asked Jesus, he chose this one. He could have asked for a 'get out of jail free' miracle. He could have asked that Jesus take on his disciples, or suggested Jesus challenge Herod's ruling. He could have ensured Jesus knew the struggle he was in the middle of because of the role he had played. But I don't think any of these thoughts entered John's head. He had lived a life consumed by anonymity, and his greatest desire was that people would come to know, trust and follow Jesus.

Jesus responds to John's question with these words: 'Go and tell John what you have seen and heard: the blind receive their sight, the lame walk, the lepers are cleansed, the deaf hear, the dead are raised, the poor have good news brought to them. And blessed is anyone who takes no offence at me.' (Lk 7:22–23)

John on hearing those words would have been consumed with peace. His mission was accomplished. He had succeeded in ushering the Messiah into people's lives. John knew that it was not he that people needed but Jesus. Belonging to John's Kingdom held no value for people – it was Jesus' Kingdom which offered life.

Once John's disciples had left to go back to John, Jesus addressed the crowd about John. He waited until John's followers had left before he began. Jesus knew John was an Anonymous Leader, and that he would be content with knowing their vision has been fulfilled – he did not need to hear what was about to be spoken.

The unheard affirmation

Jesus started addressing the people and then said, 'What then did you go out to see? A prophet? Yes, I tell you, and more than a prophet.' (Lk 7:26) John's status, in the words of the Messiah, was elevated beyond that of a prophet. A prophet was one of the greatest titles that could be bestowed on a spiritual leader, signifying they were sent from God, had given up everything, and were to be obedient to the Lord's leading even unto death. A prophet lived solely for the health and future of the people to whom he was sent.

Jesus says of John the Baptist, 'you are more than a prophet'. When our leadership moves toward anonymity, others are not only touched but also inspired. Our impact is honoured and lives on, even if our ears do not hear of it. John would not have known that any of his story was to be recorded, and he likely never even heard those words from Jesus' mouth.

Jesus said these words to honour John publicly, because honour is due those who are honourable. We lead with honour because we are compelled to, and the Anonymous Leader always moves in the direction of honour. Never motivated by the prospect of being honoured, but constantly seeking to honour others.

WHEN OUR LEADERSHIP MOVES IN THE DIRECTION OF ANONYMITY, THE INFLUENCE WE HAVE WILL REACH FAR BEYOND WHAT WE OURSELVES COULD HOPE TO CREATE.

Our ambition stands opposed to this. We long to be noticed, encouraged, affirmed and appreciated. These are the things that need to die. If they remain in us, our leadership will be limited by the lid of our ambition. This requires trusting God, and trusting that the efforts we give Him are not given in vain but contribute to something greater: making Jesus known.

A few weeks later we see John's life come to an end. King Herod was content to leave John alive but imprisoned, until he found himself in a predicament.

During a dinner party, Herodias' daughter danced and so impressed was Herod that he offered her anything she wanted. She consulted with her mother, and then asked for John's head on a platter. Herod, torn and traumatised by the request in front of an audience, relented. John was beheaded and his head presented to Herodias. His disciples took his body away and Jesus was told of the news. So an incredible display of what it was to lead anonymously came to a close.

John's execution was ordered as a result of a drunken party gone horribly astray. There was no final hoorah, no prison break attempt, and he was given no final words. Instead, one verse in the Bible later, John was gone. He left in the most gloriously anonymous fashion. No other death would have complemented him as much as this one. One minute he was there, the next gone. 'He must become greater; I must become less.' John had become less, to the point where he was no more – and just as his Messiah's influence was beginning to reach everyone, everywhere.

The movement toward anonymity

There is a progression in John's mission, 'He must become greater; I must become less.' Jesus' influence, presence and acclaim must continue to increase. In direct correlation, I must be increasingly able to enjoy stepping out of the way so that God's name is the one that is remembered. John's entire life reinforces this.

If we could have interviewed John in prison in those final hours and asked him what he felt was important about leading anonymously, I think he would have said something like, 'All that matters is the direction your leadership is moving in. Are you moving more away from your cause and more toward Christ's Cause? Are you laying aside that which is most important to you, in order to do that which is most important to God? Are you becoming more and more anonymous as your ambition slowly dies?' Or maybe he would have just told us to follow Jesus and everything else would make sense along the journey. Either way, John shows us the path of anonymity, and inspires us that we too can have the courage to follow.

The tendency to feel as though we have so far to go can be overwhelming. The truth is we do, but be empowered. Even John the Baptist, who epitomised Anonymous Leadership, recognised that he was not yet 'less'. He was in the process of decreasing and becoming less. The journey toward Anonymous Leadership is slow, taken over the course of a lifetime. Daily, weekly, monthly and yearly we recognise the direction our leadership needs to be moving, away from ambition and toward anonymity.

4

LOVE OR INSANITY?

The love of four Anonymous Leaders

I imagine it to be a warm day as the men navigated their way through the crowd. A buzz was in the air because the healer was in town. Rumoured to be a Rabbi gone rogue, a prophet announcing the end, the reports were conclusive: this man could heal. And their friend, who lay on the mat they carried, needed healing. They had taken a huge risk to collect him and pick him up, to be seen with him threatened their social standing in the community. This was of no concern to the men, however – what they were doing was a good thing and so far no-one else was being hurt or upset by it.

As they approached the house, it was clear that they had missed His arrival – the crowd surrounding the home made it clear that He was now inside. A pang of frustration rippled across the four friends as they looked to their friend lying on the mat. They thought their plan was dashed; they'd never get inside that house. Then, in a flash of brilliance, they hurriedly carried the man to the steps behind the house.

As they walked past a window they saw Him, the one they called Jesus. He was sitting in the centre of the room, surrounded by the Pharisees and the Sadducees and other faces they recognised from the community. They stumbled up the steps leading to the roof, working hard not to fall off or drop their friend.

ANONYMOUS LEADERSHIP LEADS US TO PLACES WHERE WE DON'T KNOW WHAT TO DO NEXT, AND WE FIND OURSELVES DRIVEN THERE BY LOVE FOR OTHERS. A LOVE THAT IS FREE OF SELFISH AMBITION AND CONSUMED BY A CAUSE.

So what were they to do?

While their plan seemed thwarted, the men's passion and commitment weren't. Confidently, and I suspect relying on their sense of invincibility, they started to dig into the roof. It had never been done before, and everyone would likely think they were crazy. But what other option did they have? Their friend had never been able to walk and if this Jesus could heal, He needed to meet their friend.

As Jesus sat teaching, dirt began to fall onto His shoulders and then on the floor around him. Soon it was clear that the first ever sunroof was about to be installed in the house. Those in the centre of the room backed away as the small hole began to grow. While all of the teachers of the law became infuriated, Jesus waited knowingly. I like to think He sat there smirking, realising what no-one else had yet.

Once the hole was big enough, the men took the cords that held together their outer garments and tied these to a corner of the mat. Once secure, their crippled friend was lowered through the ceiling. A hush settled over the crowd and out onto the street.

The text in Mark chapter 2 says, 'When He saw their faith, He said to the paralytic, "Son, your sins are forgiven."' As I read this, I feel somewhat let down by the anti-climax of the story. They came all that way, with all that effort, for that!

The significance of Jesus' words is lost in our culture, however. Jesus was surrounded by those who taught the law and held to a firm belief that being encumbered in any way was due to a sin in your life or your family's past. With this in mind, Jesus forgave the man, which only served to agitate the teachers of the law. They began muttering to themselves about the inappropriateness of what Jesus had done. 'Only God can forgive sins,' they said.

Then Jesus delivers the knockout blow in glorious fashion. 'Why are you thinking these things? Which is easier: to say to this paralysed man, "Your sins are forgiven," or to say, "Get up, take your mat and walk"? But I want you to know that the Son of Man has authority on earth to forgive sins.' (Mk 2:9–10)

The tension in the room would have been palpable. Jesus said to the man, 'I tell you, get up, take your mat and go home.' What a show stopper! If the man walked, Jesus' message of this coming Kingdom of Heaven would be validated. The man got up, grabbed his mat and walked out in front of everyone! The Kingdom of Heaven was breaking in.

As all this unfolded, four Anonymous Leaders sat on the roof. Love had driven them there, and they had front row seats to what Jesus did. But their names are not recorded. We don't know if they had to pay for the roof, or if they were arrested for what they did. We don't even know what happened between them and their healed friend. They were anonymous. I like that we don't know what happened to them. They received no thanks, glory or public acclaim. They weren't the stars of the show. Jesus was.

ANONYMOUS LEADERSHIP IS DRIVEN BY LOVE TO MAKE JESUS THE STAR OF THE SHOW IN OTHER PEOPLE'S LIVES.

This is a difficult aspect of the path a leader takes – a path littered with disappointment, humility and misunderstanding, and accompanied by a strong possibility of being taken for granted, used and ostracised. Its reward, however, is extravagant – providing a leader seeks to desire influence for the benefit of others.

The Anonymous Leader gets a front row seat watching God change lives and transform this world, and this is an unbeatable experience. The four friends of the paralytic man embodied Anonymous Leadership as they carried their friend through the crowd and onto the roof, and then lowered him through the hole. They watched as Jesus healed him and advanced His Kingdom. They were driven to such a feat because they loved him, and trusted Jesus was as good as they thought He was.

These Anonymous Leaders modelled for us what it looks like to influence the world by making Christ seen with greater clarity. While their names are not remembered, their role in history is. What a wonderful salute to those otherwise forgotten.

How love plays out

A few years ago, God spoke to me as loudly as He ever has – not with an audible voice but with an unmistakable impression. I'd just attended the Global Leadership Summit and heard Pranitha Timothy speak of her plight against the Indian sex trade. I was to travel to Cambodia in a few weeks and in preparation was reading *The Road of Lost Innocence* by Somaly Mam. I came home from the Summit and sat on the couch reading more of the horrors that took place in the brothels of Cambodia.

As I attempted to get my head around the culture I was to encounter, God apprehended me.

'The same issue exists in your city. It's time for you to do something about it.'

Surprised and challenged, I committed to exploring the situation. I assembled a team from the names God put on my heart and we went to work.

The team worked well and we developed a clear picture of the state of affairs in our city. This led to me approaching two gifted and strong young women, both excellent leaders in their own right, and asking them how they would feel about creating and leading this new ministry.

They both asked for time to pray and think, but a short while later they both agreed to it. The ministry we created helps, supports and loves women who are lonely, hurt, full of shame and desperate for hope. It requires Anonymous Leadership for it to be successful. Everything we do is about God calling those women into His Kingdom. The ministry has been operating for a couple of years now and continues to go from strength to strength.

Recently, I found myself in a conversation with someone from outside of this ministry, who told me how the ministry came to be and how it had developed.

It was fascinating to listen as they shared how the dream had come to be. As they told the story, I waited to see what would be said of more recent events. As they concluded, I realised they had missed someone – me! I wasn't in the story, not even as an anonymous mention.

As I reflected on that, I realised what a beautiful thing that was. The only important thing about that ministry is what God is doing in our city, through the lives of young women in need. It makes no difference if I'm part of the story or not, because it's God's story. The honour for me isn't in being named in the story but in God inviting me to be a part of it.

This was summed up best via the final words this person spoke in their recounting of the story: 'Isn't God good!' Indeed God is good. I thank God that I have been forgotten from that story, and that the founding person is identified as Jesus Christ. It is His name that will continue on long after mine is forgotten. As long as that happens, God's influence continues along with it.

ANONYMOUS LEADERSHIP CHALLENGES OUR INTENTIONS. OUR SOLE INTENTION SHOULD BE TO MAKE CHRIST KNOWN, AND ANY INFLUENCE WE ARE GIVEN IS SO WE CAN ACHIEVE THIS FOR GOD'S SAKE. THIS IS THE REASON WE ARE INVITED TO STAND ON A LEADERSHIP PLATFORM. LEADING EFFECTIVELY FROM THE PLATFORM REQUIRES THE LAYING DOWN OF OUR OWN INTENTIONS, CHOOSING TO BECOME LESS SO THAT SOMEONE ELSE CAN BECOME MORE. THE ONLY FORCE STRONG ENOUGH TO MAKE THIS POSSIBLE IS LOVE.

Loving God and the things God loves, frees us from our ambitious intentions. In encountering God's love, we become free of the need to self-preserve or self-promote. By loving God and leading those who follow, we become secure in becoming less, as the God we lead for increases.

The paradox of leadership

Christian leadership is a paradox. Denny Gunderson, who wrote *The Leadership Paradox*, quotes Oswald Chambers, who says, 'The test of our spiritual life is the power to descend.' We are misled when we believe that leadership is about becoming more powerful. Effective leadership is the opposite.

The Anonymous Leader's desire is to use their power to descend. If directed downwards, power, by its nature, must be released and dispersed. It's like stomping on an empty sealed plastic bottle. If the air within is compressed, it has to escape somewhere. This happens as the bottle repels the stomping foot upwards, or the impact blows the lid off or fractures the structure of the bottle.

WHEN WE APPLY DOWNWARD PRESSURE TO THE POWER OUR LEADERSHIP HAS, OTHERS WILL BENEFIT AS THE POWER IS DISPERSED.

An Anonymous Leader's primary role is to increase the holistic wellbeing in other people's lives. A leader does this because the one they follow is defined by it. As a friend of mine said, 'It is important to us because it is important to Him.' If this isn't important to you, the distance that has grown in your relationship to Christ is in urgent need of attention because, without attention, this dynamic will have a detrimental impact on your leadership.

The Anonymous Leader chooses to use his power to descend so that others are empowered to live holistically well lives. God is the only one who can enable a person to live a holistically well life. So, as a leader, you must be constantly creating space for God to move through your leadership. If you become too great in the eyes of the person you are leading, they will never seek God, which means they will never be whole. You are the signpost that points people toward God, and a signpost cannot afford to take up any of the road. We need to diminish to the point that we are merely signs pointing others to Christ. That is what we are truly empowered to do. This is what it means to descend, to use your power for God's glory, and to truly steward the influence God has given you.

It is a responsibility of the Anonymous Leader to help people take ownership of their own lives – to know who they are and what they are called to contribute. Everyone has something to contribute and it is the leader's role to help that person offer it to the world.

> NO LONGER IS LEADERSHIP ABOUT HOW FAR A LEADER CAN TRAVEL IN PURSUIT OF THEIR AMBITIONS. INSTEAD, LEADERSHIP IS ABOUT HOW FAR A LEADER CAN ENABLE OTHERS TO TRAVEL IN PURSUIT OF THEIR GOD-GIVEN CAUSE.

Stirred out of love

Well into His ministry, Jesus overhears a conversation His disciples were having with one another, discussing who would inherit the most honoured seat in heaven. Jesus seized the opportunity and reprimanded them, saying, 'You know that the rulers of the Gentiles lord it over them, and their great ones are tyrants over them. It will not be so among you; but whoever wishes to be great among you must be your servant, and whoever wishes to be first among you must be your slave; just as the Son of Man came not to be served but to serve, and to give His life as a ransom for many.' (Mt 20:25–28) The power of the phrase 'It will not be so among you' reveals that to follow Jesus is to embrace all that it means to be anonymous.

> CHRIST ALWAYS LEADS US TOWARD ANONYMITY AND AWAY FROM AMBITION, AND WE FOLLOW BECAUSE WE ARE MOVED BY LOVE.

Paul explains what love is when he wrote to the Church in Corinth (1 Cor 13). Each adjective he uses is a selfless directive toward becoming anonymous. Love is patient, he says, which involves the putting aside of our own agendas. Love is kind, meaning that I step away from myself and respond with warmth. Love does not boast, so I cannot love if I am consumed by myself. Love is the action of sacrifice and the commitment to another. It is love that compels a leader to serve those she cannot benefit from, and it is because of love that a leader first starts to lead.

WHEN A PERSON BEGINS TO LEAD, HE IS TOUCHED BY A NEED AND RESPONDS WITH LOVE. THAT LOVE, IF HE NURTURES IT AND HOLDS ONTO IT, HOLDS HIM TO THE STATUS OF SERVANT. IF WE MEASURE OUR LEADERSHIP AGAINST PAUL'S WORDS OF LOVE, WE CAN SEE IF IT IS INDEED ANONYMOUS, OR IF IT IS AMBITION MASKED BY ANONYMITY.

Paul says, 'love is patient; love is kind; love is not envious or boastful or arrogant or rude. It does not insist on its own way; it is not irritable or resentful; it does not rejoice in wrongdoing, but rejoices in the truth. It bears all things, believes all things, hopes all things, endures all things.' (1 Cor 13:4–7) Your leadership needs to mirror these virtues and define your interactions and motives.

The joy of leadership

Many years ago I received an excited phone call from Dan, who was one of the youth leaders I'd been mentoring and discipling. His voice exploded on the phone as he told me about what had just happened. 'You know you're always telling us to talk to people about Jesus and you're always challenging and encouraging us to? Well, I never had because I was too scared. But today I was talking to a friend who was sharing that she was in a bad way. I found myself telling her about God. Ha! Can you believe that? I still can't. I even invited her to church and told her that I'd be praying for her. I finally get it now. What you've been helping me to work out. It feels so good. I'm going to do more of this now. It's amazing.'

I couldn't wipe the smile from my face. The fruit of one's leadership is revealed in the lives of others, as they impact the world around them. I was overcome with joy; Dan was becoming the leader God had called him to become.

TO LEAD ANONYMOUSLY IS TO FORFEIT THE LIMELIGHT IN EXCHANGE FOR A DEEP SENSE OF JOY THAT GOD IS AT WORK IN THE MIDST OF YOUR INFLUENCE. WHILE YOU MIGHT PLANT A SEED, GOD MAKES IT GROW AND BEAR MUCH FRUIT.

By becoming less, the Anonymous Leader becomes more – not in power, status or position, but in their fulfilment of what it means to lead people to Christ. The ultimate test that faces all who desire to become an Anonymous Leader is in developing wisdom, integrity, resilience, humility and security; a mature character. These core leadership attributes are what compel a leader to be able to step aside, allowing those who are called to step into the role for which God has prepared for them.

The Anonymous Leader chooses to become less so that someone else can become more of who they were created to be. Love is what enables this to happen, the fruit of which is a deep joy and contentment.

PART I SUMMARY

Leadership is positive intentional influence that serves people in moving them towards a preferred future. A Christian leader grows in effectiveness as their influence reduces in direct correlation with God's influence increasing in a follower's life.

Christian leadership is a contradiction in terms that Jesus reconciles through His interactions with people. He came, representing a Cause, which He invited others to join. The Cause was God's Kingdom that promised to redefine everything for those who participated in it.

Jesus' leadership encouraged anonymity – influencing others so that through that influence they might see God and the life He is offering more clearly. The downside of this for a leader may seem to be the risk of being forgotten, overlooked, or taken for granted. The Anonymous Leader, however, embraces this as a sign that their leadership is more anonymous than ambitious.

Love is what motivates a leader to be willing to forsake the glory and credit and humbly serve – it is the well from which a leader draws to lead people consistently and at times thanklessly. It is a love from God received and a love for others given.

As an Anonymous Leader, your goal is to become hidden in Christ – transparent so that Christ can be seen in your life. This can only happen when we understand the gift of influence we have been given. This influence is not something we earned or deserved, but a gift bestowed upon us by God to serve His people with.

The platform is the best metaphor to explore this, because God has given every leader a platform from which to steward his or her influence. The size, presence or notoriety of the platform is up to God's sovereign will, and is not the determining factor in evaluating leadership success or impact. Understanding the properties of the platform and how best to live on it – the topics of the chapters in part II – is what makes a leader's influence both sustainable and profoundly powerful and significant. This all takes place as a leader grows into the realisation that it is God's Kingdom they are building and Christ's Cause they are furthering.

PART II
THE PLATFORM

5

CLOAKS AND PLATFORMS

PEOPLE SPILLED OUT onto the street. No-one could fathom what had just taken place. One moment they were praying, eating, talking and reminiscing; the next moment, all heaven had broken loose.

The room they had been residing in, owned by a wealthy friend, was tucked away in a non-descript building in the heart of Jerusalem. Just over a month ago, those in the room had all witnessed the ascension of their Leader, Messiah, Lord and Saviour. Jesus had left them, after giving them instructions to go and make the whole world disciples. He had promised to be with them always and then, ironically, left. He must have meant that He was coming back soon, but they were unsure when.

As they sat in fear of the Jewish authorities – or worse, the Roman soldiers – they did the only thing they could. Jesus had taught them how to pray so they began, praising God and seeking His Kingdom.

That's when it happened. 'Suddenly a sound like the blowing of a violent wind came from heaven and filled the whole house where they were sitting. They saw what seemed to be tongues of fire that separated and came to rest on each of them. All of them were filled with the Holy Spirit and began to speak in other tongues as the Spirit enabled them.' (Acts 2:2–4) These men had walked in the shadow of their Rabbi, Jesus, for three years but this was unlike anything they had seen or heard. Instantly, their fear was gone, replaced with a confidence, a power, to advance the Kingdom of God. With this new assurance, those in the room poured out of the house and into the festive street.

At that same time, the city was celebrating the Jewish festival Pentecost, also known as the Feast of Shavuot. The feast took place 50 days after the feast of Passover, which was when Jesus had been crucified. On that morning in the temple, the Priests read from Exodus, Ezekiel, Habakkuk and Ruth – readings that depicted the times in Jewish history when God had done a new thing through fire, a roaring wind and voice.

While Shavuot was being celebrated in the temple, God was doing something new again in the city of Jerusalem. As the Priests in the temple read from the Scriptures about how God had moved previously, The Holy Spirit descended on the disciples in a room close by. God filled that room and those in it with His power. He was saying again to the world that He chooses to be among them, as He expands upon what has previously been done.

The scene was brilliantly orchestrated by God to create a movement that would become the church. The men and women filled with the Holy Spirit spilled out of the room and made their way to the temple steps. A great commotion ensued, accompanied with great confusion.

Jews who had gathered from all the nations identified this group as Galileans – locals who were speaking in foreign tongues to praise God and prophesy. Some thought the group had had too much to drink, but others realised something of God was taking place. Jerusalem was being infected by a new movement of God, which left those observing it astonished and perplexed.

If you were a leader in that room, what would you have thought? What would you have done? Something inside a leader stirs them to bring order to chaos, to bring direction to disorientation and clarity to confusion, and to offer a way forward. The leader who stood to bring order to the chaos was Peter, one of the remaining 11 followers of Jesus.

He didn't have a plan – this was new territory for everyone – but he had just been filled with the power to offer the people a vision. Peter, as we will soon discover, had developed into an Anonymous Leader.

Understanding the platform

The 14th verse of the second chapter of Acts is the fulcrum of our story: 'Then Peter stood up with the Eleven, raised his voice and addressed the crowd.'

As Peter stood up, he realised he had been given influence to affect the chaotic situation. He had been given the opportunity to transform the chaos into clarity. So Peter ventures onto an elevated step, providing him a platform from which to speak.

Michael Hyatt, in his book *Platform: Get Noticed in a Noisy World*, says 'The word *platform* itself is a metaphor for the stage ... a stage on which you are elevated above the crowd. It makes it possible for everyone in the audience to see you ... It enables you to be heard above the roar of the crowd.' This was what Peter had stepped onto, a platform – the same space every Christian leader occupies. It is the allocated space where a person chooses to use their influence with intention, for the good of others.

We realise some things about Peter as he steps up. First, he wants to honour God by ensuring that those who were confused become clear about what God is doing. Second, he wants to serve the people, by offering some explanation as to what is going on. Third, something within him draws him to the platform to lead the other 10. The other disciples stood with him, but Peter's courage, boldness and eagerness caused action from which change could then take place.

Peter was the most strategic person to speak in the situation. He had journeyed with Jesus for three years, and was one of the first to follow Him. He was great at speaking his mind and had the courage to do it in a hostile setting. God had orchestrated it so wonderfully. When leadership was required, Peter was there to offer it. Peter wasn't forcing his way into the spotlight – he found himself there and then used the spotlight to highlight the work of Christ; the mark of an Anonymous Leader. He had stepped onto a platform that God gave him, having prepared it for him to occupy. This is the first aspect of Anonymous Leadership.

WHOSE PLATFORM ARE YOU STANDING ON? IS IT A GOD-GIVEN PLATFORM OR IS IT A SELF-MADE PLATFORM?

Self-made platforms

A self-made platform isn't a bad thing; it just isn't possible to lead anonymously from it. The foundation of the self-made platform is ourselves, which is why this type of platform is more like a stage. We want to occupy the stage so that others will look at us, follow, like, talk about, admire, pay, worship or idolise us. We don't like to own up to the dark reality dwelling within us, but it's there.

INSIDE EVERY LEADER IS A SEED OF SELF-AMBITION THAT WANTS TO BE THE STAR ON THE STAGE.

I feel ashamed owning up to it, but several years ago I caught myself ambitiously pursuing the stage. Before creating my current leadership blog (www.ralphmayhew.com), I had a more general-purpose blog I would post to. I was keen for more visitors and one day came upon an idea that might achieve this.

I would run a competition that offered prize money to the person who could most creatively answer the following: if you had $xxxxx, what would you do to change the world? The winner would then use that prize money to change the world. I'd document it on my blog, people would be empowered and resourced and, best of all, people would be helped. The idea seemed plausible, so I approached a couple of high-profile people to judge the competition.

These people had a much larger profile than I in the blogging world and, to my surprise, they agreed in principle to be judges. I then approached some others and asked if they would be interested in financially backing it. This was the first time I'd done anything like this, but after a few weeks things were in place. The only thing left for me to do was to launch the competition nationwide.

As I prayerfully considered the project and the support people were offering me, the weight of responsibility increased. I recall thinking, *This is a lot to take on; what if it doesn't come off? What if it's a flop? What if someone just takes the money? What if the ideas people enter are impossible or disappointing? What if no-one enters or, worse, just one person?* As these doubts began to escalate in my mind I heard the whisper of God, a whisper so faint I was lucky not to have missed it all together. It was a single thought: *Whose Kingdom are you building?*

The competition was a new, fresh and creative idea that would help a lot of people, and maybe inspire others to do the same. How was this not building God's Kingdom? Despite this, the Holy Spirit's impression remained: *Whose Kingdom are you building?* The more I thought about it, the more uncomfortable I felt.

Everything I had planned looked like it was furthering the Cause of Christ, including my intent and desire. The only problem was I was standing on a stage not a platform. The stage exists for only one reason: to pursue the ambition of influence. I had created, driven and set up my idea. I knew it would make a great deal of difference in this world but I had conveniently overlooked the personal benefit it would create for me. In all honesty, this was the real reason I was going to do it.

I am still embarrassed about my intentions. I was willing to use what others gave me to increase my influence. The Anonymous Leader doesn't need to do this – God provides the opportunity through us for His influence to take effect. Forcing or manipulating this only serves to damage what He has entrusted to us. When I looked back on that project, it was clearly the work of my hands and not God's.

THE ANONYMOUS LEADER WAITS FOR THE PLATFORM TO BE PRESENTED TO HIM BY GOD. AT THE SAME TIME, HE REALISES THAT IT IS GOD'S ORCHESTRATION THAT IS NOW INVITING HIM ON TO THE PLATFORM TO OCCUPY IT. THIS DOESN'T MEAN THAT BEING SMART, CREATIVE OR INNOVATIVE AREN'T IMPORTANT, QUITE THE OPPOSITE. THESE THINGS ARE EXPRESSIONS OF THE KINGDOM OF GOD. IT MEANS THAT THE ANONYMOUS LEADER NEEDS TO WEED OUT SELF-AMBITION AND TRUST GOD IN WHAT HE DESIRES TO DO WITH OUR EFFORTS.

The platform of your leadership

Peter was an Anonymous Leader and, as he stood up with the rest of the disciples and raised his voice, people were spellbound – not only enthralled by his words, but also captivated by the Holy Spirit. As a result, 3,000 people chose to be baptised and join this new movement. The church was born.

The Anonymous Leader does not lead to gain more influence; he leads so those who follow might be more influenced. Peter didn't stand up to increase his influence. He stood so the influence that was upon him, given him by the Holy Spirit, would influence those gathered.

Secular leadership is about trying to gain more influence, and this has been verified by numerous well-written books on the subject. Biblical leadership is not.

BIBLICAL LEADERSHIP IS ABOUT ENSURING THOSE WHO ARE LED ARE BEING SHAPED, CULTIVATED, ENRICHED, CHALLENGED AND DIRECTED BY THE ONE WHOM THE LEADER LEADS ON BEHALF OF.

A helpful indicator to evaluate your position on this scale is to ask yourself, 'Do I want more and more influence so that I can lead and affect the lives of more people?' If you answer yes, maybe the platform you're standing on is actually a stage. Perhaps your leadership is moving toward self-ambition rather than anonymity.

Making the distinction between the two can be difficult. But remember – the Anonymous Leader does not lead to gain more influence; she leads that those who follow might be more influenced. Now, you would be right in thinking, *How can I lead if I cannot influence?* This is what makes the distinction difficult. The differentiating element, however, is the direction your leadership is moving in. If your leadership is moving in the direction of wanting or needing more influence to do your job better, to have a greater impact, or to fulfil the goals before you, you will be forced to dig deeper into yourself, to try to acquire a larger platform, to cajole people into following you. That direction of leadership is about establishing ourselves as leaders and that is rooted in self-ambition.

In contrast to this stands the Anonymous Leader who is prepared to die; who does not lead in order to be special, but just the opposite. She leads in order to become nothing. She leads so that those who would dare to follow – because of the influence she has been lent – can discover a greater cause behind her, which brings transformation to their lives.

THE ANONYMOUS LEADER STEPS ONTO THE PLATFORM SO THAT WHEN THOSE NOT ON THE PLATFORM LOOK AT HER THEY SEE THE ONE WHO STANDS BEHIND HER; THE ONE WHO GAVE HER THE PLATFORM TO STAND ON IN THE FIRST PLACE. THE ANONYMOUS LEADER'S ROLE IS TO BE THE FOCAL POINT THROUGH WHICH PEOPLE SEE WHAT GOD DESIRES TO DO IN THEIR LIVES.

Why is this not self-ambitious? It's because God bids us 'come and die'. Of course, the leader who brings that message may not be too favourable among those who are considering following. To follow this kind of leadership requires an indwelling of the Spirit of God, which evokes a servant heart to give all for the Cause of Christ.

This was the platform that Peter stepped onto and remained on for the duration of his life. The idea of the platform can revolutionise our understanding of leadership.

The general understanding of leadership is that a person gets asked to lead, is promoted to a leadership role, or one day finds themselves intentionally influencing others. When this occurs people might say that person 'has leadership'. I've said it – we all say it. A limitation of this approach is this person now has resting on their lives some metaphorical invisible cloak of leadership which they take wherever they go. It's theirs, just like the elven cloak given to Frodo in *Lord of the Rings*. They own it and have it to do with what they want. They can take it off and put it on as they please to accomplish what they want. When this idea is owned by and plays itself out in the life of an emerging leader, the likelihood of foolishness leading to disqualification increases.

The danger of cloaked leadership

For many years I have worked with emerging leaders and seen the limitations of this understanding of leadership. The culture in which many young adults live powerfully entices them toward alcohol, smoking, drugs, gambling, violence and sexual exploits. This is not always isolated to young adults either. This powerful culture can turn a God-fearing leader into a self-gratifying mess. It happens – not just to emerging leaders but also pastors (who have marital affairs, for example). Worship leaders become all wrapped up in their own ego, lay leaders pilfer unaccounted funds, elders abuse their power for personal agendas, volunteers choose to disregard standards they previously agreed to, and so on. It looks different in every church, but the bottom line is the same. Broken people have been called to lead, and they wear that title, regardless of what they do – even if they are running toward self-ambitious and destructive ends.

When a leader engages in behaviour that contradicts their leadership expectations, a conversation happens, or at least should. The leader in question sits down with their supervisor and is asked about what they've been doing. In my experience, what often follows is an argument, where both the leader and the supervisor argue about whether the behaviour was wrong.

When challenged about the amount of alcohol they have drunk over the last few weekends, or some other behaviour conducted outside of *ministry time*, an emerging leader frequently offers the same responses. 'People are talking about you,' might be what the supervisor says. 'Do you think you're setting a good example?' To which the leader says something like, 'What's the harm? There wasn't anyone I lead present. Besides, I hardly drank anything. It's no big deal.' Conversations like this are never productive and often create more confusion and conflict.

The issue is, this emerging leader understands his leadership as belonging to him. In his eyes, it is something that he can determine the appearance of, depending on how he's feeling and what's going on for him. He wears the cloak when he's on duty, and hangs it up when he's not.

LEADERSHIP IS NOT SOMETHING A PERSON OWNS, WEARS OR DOES WHAT THEY LIKE WITH. LEADERSHIP IS A PLATFORM – A GOD-GIVEN PLATFORM TO SEE THE CAUSE OF CHRIST PREVAIL – AND THIS CHANGES THE WAY WE CAN TALK ABOUT LEADERSHIP.

Honouring the platform

It is convoluted to say to a person what they can and can't do as a leader. (Not to mention we all have the ability to twist priorities, situations, words and rules to fit our circumstances.) The conversation seems doomed from the outset. A new way of looking at this is required.

Instead of putting expectations or requirements on the leader, what if we put them on the platform? By this I mean, when a person takes on a leadership responsibility, they relocate their entire life to the platform.

Choosing to occupy a leadership platform requires them to accept and embrace the expectations of the platform.

Each leadership platform has certain requirements, which anybody occupying the platform must honour in all environments. If you cannot honour the platform, you are not fit or ready to be given or maintain any leadership responsibility.

I need to be clear and careful here so these two metaphors of leadership can be seen for what they are.

Moving away from the cloak of leadership

Let's go back to the cloak metaphor for a moment. When a person is asked to step into a leadership position, they are given a cloak. The cloak enables them to be respected, well loved, trusted, wise and a person of integrity. As they go about the role asked of them, they intentionally influence people, and empower, equip and serve them. Then the shift finishes. They hang up their cloak, go home as a non-leader, and do what they like. They return the following day, put the cloak on and go back to leading.

What this leader doesn't realise is that no-one sees them take the cloak off. In everyone's perceptions, they are still a leader, regardless of where they are. They are still expected to be the wise, trusted, influential, caring role model of integrity that they were when they were wearing the cloak. Frequently, the downfall of an emerging leader is they don't understand themselves in the same way as they've asked others to understand them.

This is the trap emerging leaders find themselves ensnared by: cloak on, I'm a leader; cloak off, I'm not. Their misstep is caused by the way they were invited into leadership and the manner in which leadership is talked about and understood.

They are being set up, so that when the spotlight is on them they are all that is needed from a leader, but when the spotlight goes out, it doesn't matter who they are. This is a broken and incomplete understanding of leadership.

Leading always from the platform

A redeemed and complete understanding of leadership is established when a leader steps into a position of influence by being invited onto a platform and is informed that this platform is God's, on loan to them. Their task is to steward God's influence as best they can so that God's best takes place in people's lives. They are told that it doesn't matter what they are doing, what time the clock says or whether they are out with friends or home alone – they are on the platform of leadership. It is not an option to leap off the platform, and then jump back on. To leap off is to relinquish the opportunities the platform provides. We are not invited onto it because of a role we do, but because of who we are; not for a time, but for a lifetime.

This leader is then told that the entirety of their life now exists on the platform. As we live on this platform, everything we do becomes an offering to God, an act of worship which God will decide the use of.

The Apostle Paul urged the men and women he was writing to 'in view of God's mercy, to offer your bodies as a living sacrifice, holy and pleasing to God – this is your true and proper worship.' (Rom 12:1) Paul understood what life on the platform looked like. When this is embraced, everything comes to be an expression of leadership. This is the life of the Anonymous Leader.

IT BECOMES CLEAR TO THE ANONYMOUS LEADER THAT THEIR IDENTITY AS A LEADER IS NOT TIED TO THEIR ROLE – TO WHAT THEY DO OR HOW MUCH THEY DO IT. THEIR IDENTITY IS TIED TO THEIR

CALLING, AND TO THE ONE WHO CALLS THEM. IF THEY ARE CALLED TO LEAD, THEY ARE CALLED TO THE PLATFORM UPON WHICH THEY WILL LIVE ALL OF THEIR LIFE. FOR THE PLATFORM IS WHERE EVERYTHING CAN BE SEEN, AND WHERE EVERYONE CAN SEE.

The God-given platform determines what a leader's life needs to look like – not what a person feels like after they think they have stopped leading for the day. The leadership platform belongs to God. It is the platform upon which He influences lives. To live consistently on the platform requires wisdom, integrity, resilience, humility and our security. If we choose to occupy the platform – that is, if we choose to lead – a responsibility accompanies that. The platform is borrowed ground; it is God's platform, which means even when we stand on it, God is the one who is represented. The Anonymous Leader lives and breathes to make known the owner and giver of the platform.

A royal priesthood

Years after that incredible day of Pentecost, Peter still occupied the platform as he wrote to God's elect. They were exiles scattered throughout the provinces of Pontus, Galatia, Cappadocia, Asia and Bithynia, and they included both Jews and Gentiles who had become Christians. In these small outlying towns and provinces, they were fearful of the Roman Empire as it threatened to sweep through their lands.

Peter knows this and writes to encourage them. In so doing, he discovers divisions between the Jew and Gentile believers. He writes to help them understand who they now are in Christ. Peter's letter builds to these beautiful timeless words: 'But you are a chosen people, a royal priesthood, a holy nation, God's special possession, that you may declare the praises of Him who called you out of darkness into His wonderful light. Once you were not a people, but now you are the people of God; once you had not received mercy, but now you have received mercy.' (1 Pt 2:9–10)

The difficulty we have, of course, is that while we can be struck by the romantic language of a 'royal priesthood', we are not familiar with the concept. Peter's audience were, of course. They knew that the priests were responsible for the sacrificial system, appointed by God to steward the forgiveness of sins and to welcome humankind into that exchange. The priests advocated and interceded for the people. They were set aside to do this. When Peter tells the exiles they are now the royal priesthood, he is helping them understand their role is to intercede for those who are not yet forgiven. They are now ambassadors of God's grace and hope. Peter enables them see that they too, like he has for all these years, stand upon a platform that the world is looking at.

He confirms this in his next few words: 'Dear friends, I urge you, as foreigners and exiles, to abstain from sinful desires, which wage war against your soul. Live such good lives among the pagans that, though they accuse you of doing wrong, they may see your good deeds and glorify God on the day He visits us.' (1 Pt 2:11–12) He wants them to understand that, by finding their salvation in Jesus Christ, they were given a platform upon which to live their lives. Peter charges them to live with such goodness that people would look at them and see what God is like and be moved to glorify Him. Peter is revealing to these Jewish and Gentile believers that they are to intentionally influence this world for the Cause of Christ. They are now a royal priesthood, and need to live and act like one.

In Australia where I am writing this, we have what feels like a distant tie to royalty, given Australia is still in the Commonwealth and has a monarchy, whilst having its own parliament and prime minister. I was, however, born in England where the royal family reside. In England, the royal family has a far superior standing in the minds of the people, for better or for worse. But if we borrow from their perspective, we can gain a greater understanding of what Peter wants us to grasp.

The English have certain expectations of how the royal family needs to present themselves, including how they need to behave and what values they need to embody. When they fulfil what is expected, people are assured of certain virtues, such as stability, security, strength and hope. These virtues are needed by the people and they expect them to be reinforced by everything the royal family does – from their public appearances, to the way they speak, to their titles and stances on certain social issues.

When a member of the royal family acts contrary to these expectations – for example, when they are photographed in questionable scenarios – something significant occurs. The trust invested in them is breached, and the breach causes people to doubt what they were asked to trust in. And because the people have come to rely on that which they were asked to trust in, this breach of trust also results in a feeling of insecurity.

The member of the royal family could perhaps argue they weren't doing anything wrong, just like a leader might argue that they are not doing anything wrong. Their behaviour, however, is outside of what they have asked people to expect of them, and these expectations are associated with the platform they occupy. This behaviour, while not wrong, shakes the virtues they have asked people to rely on, believe in them for and trust. Honouring the platform is essential because of what is lost if it is dishonoured.

Transparency on the platform

By leading, you are choosing to live on the platform. When you stand on the platform in front of people, you are inviting them to follow you. You are seeking to intentionally influence them for a Cause, and representing to them something they can trust in and give themselves to.

WHEN YOU STAND ON THE PLATFORM, YOU GIVE THOSE WHO FOLLOW YOU STABILITY, SECURITY, HOPE AND STRENGTH. WHEN A LEADER BEHAVES CONTRARY TO THE EXPECTATION THE PLATFORM CREATES, THEY COMPROMISE ALL THE THINGS THEY HAVE USED TO ESTABLISH INFLUENCE AND TRUST WITH THEIR FOLLOWERS.

Putting on and taking off leadership like a cloak is a broken understanding of what leadership is. Leadership is a platform upon which we are to live. It is God-given, and we are invited onto it. As we live on that platform, people follow us because they trust in the platform upon which we stand. They come to trust in God because it is His platform. When we violate the integrity of the platform, we risk jeopardising the trust people have built, not just in us, but in what we stand for. The Anonymous Leader must expect that a follower will rely on transparency in every part of his life.

6

FENCING IN THE PLATFORM

Empowerment on the platform

It was getting really late and the night had been a tough one. The Youth Ministry program I led had just finished. I was relieved because it had been a disaster on so many levels. Everything from leader performance, policy adherence and vision clarity had failed in one form or another. I was frustrated and confused as to what had gone wrong.

Some young people were struggling with serious issues, while some leaders had been underwhelming. Unexpected situations had arisen and the responses to these situations had violated our pre-set procedures. Despite the time, it was necessary to debrief – to discover what we needed to in order to learn from it and improve.

As the team began to discuss the various situations, I began to notice something I hadn't fully realised – our team was dysfunctional.

A leader shared how she thought it was important to make a decision and act on it, regardless of the opposite directions I had given the team.

When I mentioned that we only had three hours a week to impact these young people's lives, and shouldn't waste it talking to our leader friends, I received strong push-back. I could hardly believe what my ears were hearing.

I walked the team through a serious situation that had unfolded and, as I did so, discovered that policies we had in place had been violated because leaders were unaware of them. I felt my blood run cold.

I looked at the shambles our team was in and was attempting to calm them down when it dawned on me that we had either lost something valuable or never had it in the first place. We had a problem.

No-one knew what they were supposed to do or how they were supposed to do it, and they were killing each other because of it. Egos raged and personalities tried to 'lord' it over others. The plans we had spent hours developing and implementing – specifically for nights such as the one we had just endured – were completely disregarded. The values of individuals, when under pressure, became more important than the values we had all agreed to as a team. Regrettably many of my leaders had not understood what empowerment was and that they were empowered to lead.

Delegation or empowerment?

I find myself feeling irritated when leaders talk about delegating a responsibility. Delegation has its place but it is the lesser cousin of empowerment.

> **TO DELEGATE IS TO ASK SOMEONE TO FULFIL A TASK, BUT LIMIT THE POWER OR AUTHORITY THEY HAVE TO ACHIEVE THAT TASK. EMPOWERMENT IS TO RELINQUISH YOUR POWER AND GIVE IT TO THE PERSON YOU ASK TO DO THE TASK.**

The two are quite different and the distinguishing factor is control. Empowerment requires you to relinquish control.

A servant doesn't seek to control. Servants, by nature of their title, are powerless apart from the power given to them by their master. It is the same for us. We can claim or pursue power that is not ours by taking it inappropriately or at the expense of another. When we do this, however, we violate our status as servants in God's Kingdom. This means we stray from following Christ and building His Cause.

We may claim that this power we have taken is necessary to ensure God is glorified, but if we took it, as opposed to being given it, it's for our agenda – even if doing so makes serving the Cause easier or more achievable. We want someone to fill a roster, work harder or do a job for us. We tell ourselves it's for God's ultimate benefit so we push, coerce, manipulate, guilt or, worse, force the person into doing that task. That way, a job we needed to have accomplished is achieved. The awful downside, however, is something wonderful is lost: the opportunity for a person to freely step into the power God wants them to have.

While someone might argue, 'but the Kingdom is being built', I think Jesus would say, 'You know that the rulers of the Gentiles lord it over them, and their great ones are tyrants over them. It will not be so among you.' (Mt 20:24–26) Jesus modelled and taught that we are to invite people to share in the power He has given us, so they might serve God and not us.

OUR LEADERSHIP IS TO BE ONE OF SERVICE – AND NOT JUST SERVICE OF GOD, BUT ALSO SERVICE OF THE PEOPLE HE ENTRUSTS TO US. THIS IS WHAT LIFE AND LEADERSHIP ON THE PLATFORM NEED TO REFLECT SO YOU DON'T FALL FROM THE PLATFORM.

A proscriptive model

While studying my master's degree in leadership, I took a week-long leadership intensive with Craig Bailey. During that class, Craig gave us a tool with which we might empower people more effectively. He called it the 'Proscriptive Model of Leadership', which he had developed out of John Carver's Model of Management.

As Craig taught us how we might use the tool, I realised this had the potential to become a powerful model that might enable us to bypass those awkward and confusing confrontations about what a leader should and shouldn't do.

This Proscriptive Model of Leadership lends itself to understanding the leadership platform with greater insight and clarity. So I borrowed the model from Craig and adapted it to the idea of Anonymous Leadership. The results, I think, offer a greater understanding of how to actually lead more anonymously, as we occupy the platform. To fully benefit from this we need to use a metaphor.

As a kid I spent every weekend riding my bike out to my friend's dairy farm. We would spend the days getting up to all kinds of mischief. One of my favourite memories was watching my brother get 'clothes lined' by an electric fence while running at full pace. The red burn line from one side of his chest to the other was the envy of us all.

Electric fences are made of metal wire and charged with a voltage of electricity, giving anyone or anything that touches them a significant shock. They were used across the farm to divide up the land and confine the cattle to graze systematically from field to field. These fences ensure the cows remain in the field the farmer has chosen for them to roam in.

While the cows may find this restrictive, the farmer uses the fences to keep both the cows and the fields healthy. The fences control how much a cow eats and from where, and protects the health of each field on the farm, as well as the health and safety of each cow. The fences protect what the farmer wants to see achieved with both his cows and his fields.

Just as a field of cows is fenced, so is the leadership platform. The fences on the platform are provided by God to ensure that His people are cared for under the influence of a leader. Four fences define a leader's platform: vision, values, culture and heart. Within these fences, a leader has the freedom to do whatever they want to influence people.

Much like attempting to cross an electric fence gives you a vicious zap, crossing any one of the platform's fences (vision, values, culture and heart), will leave your leadership damaged. Doing so will compromise what God wants to achieve through your leadership on His platform. Inside of these four fences, however, is great freedom for originality, creativity and innovation to move people forward.

Are the platform's fences clear?

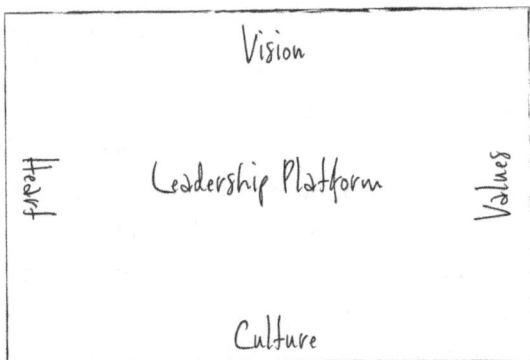

Knowing where the fences of the platform stand is an essential part of leading anonymously and with excellence. Without a clear understanding of the fences' location, we don't know what we are allowed to do or how we are to express that. My Youth Ministry team had no clarity about any of the four fences of their leadership and, as a result, didn't understand what freedom they had.

The Apostle Paul, father figure to a young Timothy, wrote to help him understand what leadership in the early church should look like. Paul pointed out to Timothy what the fences of the platform looked like. For many different reasons, Paul felt it was necessary to be clear and detailed with Timothy, while he thought about the church that Timothy pastored.

He said, 'the overseer is to be above reproach, faithful to his wife, temperate, self-controlled, respectable, hospitable, able to teach, not given to drunkenness, not violent but gentle, not quarrelsome, not a lover of money. He must manage his own family well and see that his children obey him, and he must do so in a manner worthy of full respect. (If anyone does not know how to manage his own family, how can he take care of God's church?) He must not be a recent convert ... He must also have a good reputation with outsiders.' (1 Tm 3:1–7) After speaking about overseers, Paul continues on to speak of what is to be expected of deacons. 'In the same way, deacons are to be worthy of respect, sincere, not indulging in much wine, and not pursuing dishonest gain. They must keep hold of the deep truths of the faith with a clear conscience.' (1 Tm 3:8–10)

Paul wanted to ensure that those who were given the opportunity and responsibility to intentionally influence others for the Cause of Christ knew what was expected of them. They would be held to these requirements and asked to provide reasons if they ever departed from them. Indeed, if this ever transpired, I suspect Paul's tolerance would have been short and the discussion would have concluded with the end of that leader's opportunity.

This dilemma has faced the church in every generation since. Freedom or law? Trust or advantage? Conservative or liberal? Are leaders to be given strict boundaries to adhere to, or are they to be trusted not to take advantage of very loose guidelines? If they do take advantage, are they ignored, released from leadership or redeemed?

First of all, let me clarify that there is no right answer. Second, every church falls somewhere on the scale and every point on the scale is fraught with struggle. 'It is a tension to be managed', as Andy Stanley in his Leadership Podcast says, 'and not a problem to be solved.' Third, the particulars of a situation greatly determine any action that may transpire. A course of action may work really well in one situation and fail in another. There are no guarantees.

Some churches are adamant about what a person should wear if they are performing on the stage, but far more relaxed about how they might express their sexuality off of it. Some churches are strict on what one's social life should look like, but their cultures are infected with gossip, lying and slander. No-one has it right all of the time. I'm not even sure *right* exists.

This is why life on the platform can be so confusing. God provides a platform and the Anonymous Leader occupies it, trying to live in such a way as to point others toward Christ and adopt His Cause. Yet, that leader is unsure about where the platform ceases to be the platform. They don't know where the fence is – until they cross it and receive a reprimand – unless they are told.

Staying in the field

Crossing a fence protecting the platform happens when the vision is disregarded, agreed upon values are compromised, culture is violated or our heart's motive strays.

This does not mean that our influence ceases or that we are disqualified from leadership – although these are potential outcomes. To cross a fence, however, is to claim the influence you have for yourself. It is to move toward an ambitious pursuit of influence, one where the end goal is not the Cause for which you lead, but in fact your own glorification or success.

When a fence is crossed, the Cause that we are asking people to follow is put in jeopardy. Remember – to lead is to steward the trust others place in us.

THE ANONYMOUS LEADER EXAMINES, UNDERSTANDS, HONOURS AND VALUES THAT TRUST. OUR PEOPLE HAVE ENTRUSTED US WITH SOMETHING THAT IS FAR GREATER THAN WE CAN FULLY COMPREHEND. TO TAKE THIS TRUST LIGHTLY IS TO INSULT THOSE WHOM WE LEAD. THEY TRUST US TO REPRESENT THAT WHICH WE HAVE ASKED THEM TO BUY INTO, AND MISREPRESENTING THAT HAS SEVERE CONSEQUENCES.

First, people might follow us away from the Cause and toward the self-ambition we begin to pursue. This means we have used the influence God has given us for our own gain (something the Kings in the Old Testament knew much about).

Second, people might begin to see that the direction we are leading them in is away from the Cause they signed up to. This leads to pain, misunderstanding and confusion – ultimately resulting in a struggle and eventual loss for both the follower and the leader.

Third, people might begin to think that the Cause they signed up to in the first place isn't what the leader has represented it to be. Suspicion about the Cause will grow until there is an unexplainable void between what the leader represents and what they thought the Cause was. This becomes a chasm too large to negotiate and people fall away from both the leader and the Cause.

There are a plethora of reasons a follower may choose to stop investing in the Cause for which their leader stands. But a lot of responsibility must rest on the leader, who is primarily responsible for stewarding their leadership in such a way that they stay connected to the Cause. Where the leader goes, so the followers go. This is where the fences help us.

Having a clear understanding of what each fence is increases the amount a person can be empowered to lead with freedom. As a leader – empowering others – your responsibility is to make the vision, values, culture and heart, which you wish another to adhere to, to be made as clear as possible. As an emerging leader – being empowered by a leader – your responsibility is to know exactly what vision, value, culture and heart your leader expects of you.

Once these things are clear, the emerging leader is empowered to lead – they know how they are to conduct themselves, on the platform, in a way that upholds the Cause in all they do.

The expectations created or embraced as a person begins to lead are shaped by these four fences. This dynamic is seen in the life of public figures such as sportsmen and sportswomen, politicians, businesspeople, clergy and others. We all know the feeling of hearing of another sportsperson who has disqualified themselves because of the behaviour they have exhibited off the field with recreational drugs, alcohol or violence. Or the young pop star who has used their perceived power to position themselves above the law, only to find that wasn't possible. The examples continue – the politician who has been channelling public funds into private accounts, or the clergy member who has been hiding behind a veil of trust only to be engaged in the horrors of child pornography. When we hear of such fences being crossed we are saddened, and perhaps outraged or disappointed.

We feel like this because we expected more of these people. They asked us to expect more of them by stepping onto the platform, just like Christian leaders are asking their followers to expect more of them. This is the trade-off of influence – if you are to have influence that improves the lives of others, you need to embrace, and to a large extent fulfil, these expectations (providing those expectations fall within the fences of the platform). A prominent person failing to steward their platform well affects all those who fall under the shadow of their influence. This is the cost of living on the platform, but all who do are subject to its laws.

So let's explore these four fences in more detail, so we have a better grasp of what the platform looks like and how we might occupy it with more effectiveness.

Vision

Leadership requires vision. Without direction, vision or a desired future, what might be viewed as leadership is really just the blind following a person as they wander aimlessly. Vision frames forward momentum and channels it toward a destination.

VISION IS A PICTURE GOD DEVELOPS IN US OF WHAT HE CAN MAKE POSSIBLE IN THE FUTURE.

In his brilliant book about change management, *Leading Change*, John Kotter speaks about six characteristics of an effective vision. Such a vision needs to be:

Imaginable: conveys a picture of what the future will look like. Desirable: appeals to the long-term interests of employees, customers, stockholders and others who have stake in the enterprise. Feasible: comprises reasonable, attainable goals. Focused: is clear enough to provide guidance in decision making. Flexible: is general enough to allow for individual initiative and alternative responses in light of changing conditions. Communicable: is easy to communicate; can be successfully explained within five minutes.

These are helpful distinguishers for developing a great effective vision that will equip and empower people, in contrast to a vision that will frustrate and confuse people. The ultimate question is, what is God's greatest desire for the future that He has called you to lead?

Jesus revealed God's greatest desire when He preached on a Galilean mountainside. The words are featured in the sixth chapter of Matthew, when Jesus decides to offer some clarity about how to pray:

> This, then, is how you should pray:
> 'Our Father in heaven,
> hallowed be Your name,
> Your Kingdom come,
> Your will be done,
> on earth as it is in heaven.
> Give us today our daily bread.
> And forgive us our debts,
> as we also have forgiven our debtors.
> And lead us not into temptation,
> but deliver us from the evil one.' (6:9–13)

The pivotal point of this prayer seems to be the sentence nearing the middle: 'your will be done'. What is God's greatest desire for His creation? Of the infinite choices God has at His disposal, which one enables the creation which He loves to be benefitted the most? The answer has to be found in what God has that He can give to His creation. The answer is His Kingdom.

Whatever you understand heaven to be like, it is about peace, hope, love, promise and providence in their fullness. A place where pain, sadness and grief are somehow disempowered, and we are consumed by the grace, forgiveness, generosity, encouragement, praise and worship of God. God's Kingdom is the full picture of God's restoration that He invites His creation into through Jesus Christ. 'Your Kingdom come, your will be done, on earth as it is in heaven.' May what God's Kingdom looks like, be what God's creation begins to look like – meaning our experience in God's creation would grow to become identical to our future experience in heaven, God's Kingdom.

Jesus gives us His vision of what He has in store for us – where trust in His teaching, actions and life finds its fulfilment, and we are ushered into God's reality that overpowers, and begins to change, our current reality. This was what the vision fence line of Jesus' platform looked like – a fence that Scripture encourages us to also erect around our leadership.

VISION IS A FENCE THAT PREVENTS ANYTHING IN JESUS' MINISTRY COMPROMISING GOD'S VISION. NOTHING JESUS DID OR WAS INVOLVED WITH, INSTRUCTED OR ENCOURAGED EVER CROSSED THE VISION FENCE – THE PRECEPTS OF HIS KINGDOM.

Imagine if Jesus had been in an altercation with a person and punched them, hurling abuse at them as they hit the dirt. This would have been a clear violation of the vision Jesus' platform had. If Jesus had whinged and gossiped about those Pharisees who were getting on His nerves, it would have served as another clear violation of the vision He upheld with His leadership. We would be able to recognise these violations and sniff them out, because the vision Jesus offers us of His Kingdom creates in us certain expectations of how Jesus will conduct His leadership – all of His leadership, and all of His life. The vision a leader offers does that. It creates expectations in the minds of the followers, outlines what you can trust in and promises that trust will not be violated by doing anything contrary to it.

Creating your vision

Every leader embodies a vision – it's one of the things that makes them a leader. As you assess yourself now, what vision have you bought into?

Knowing the answer to this question will help clarify the way you will lead. Be specific and accurate. These questions may help:

- What has taken hold of your heart?
- What would you be willing to give any spare moment to?
- What occupies your thoughts on a consistent basis?
- What do you feel compelled to give your own money to?
- When others don't see how important what you are doing is, what is the main thing you want to clarify with them?

The answers to these questions will help you identify the vision you have given yourself to, or help you to discover what that vision is.

Vision is only one fence that provides freedom for a leader on the platform. Let's now talk about values.

Values

'Beliefs define what you value, and what you value defines how you behave. Or in reverse, how we act shows what we value, what we value shows what we believe.' A great friend gave me that concise insight as I prepared to teach a class on this subject. Values and beliefs are in such close relationship with each other that to speak of one without the other is incomplete.

I find when an emerging leader is exploring their values, they tend to name things that close friends would immediately question. That's not bad or dishonest, it's just we don't have a clear understanding or awareness of who we are, whereas those who have some perspective (that is, those who are not in our heads) do. A gap exists between who we would like to be and who we are. The mature leader seeks to reduce this gap, by ensuring they know themselves well. Great power comes from being able to do this, and in so doing the fences of your leadership platform become clear.

If 'belief defines what you value, and what you value defines how you behave', then the most effective way to discover our values is to examine how we behave. What words do we speak? What behaviours do we have? What actions do we take? What thoughts do we have?

For example, say I said, 'I value honesty.' I might talk about it a lot, tell others to be honest, and get hurt or frustrated when others aren't; however, at the same time I might choose to lie. Even if I lie in a small way – to secure an advantage, tweak the truth to avoid some negative consequence or exaggerate on what I know to be the correct figures in order to look or feel better about my accomplishments – these things are my actions and 'how we act shows what we value, what we value shows what we believe'. I may well say I value honesty, but in fact I value honesty from others, but not from myself when it has a detrimental effect on my life.

THE ANONYMOUS LEADER NEEDS TO BE DILIGENT AND STUDIOUS WHEN IT COMES TO THE ISSUE OF VALUES. THE ULTIMATE GOAL IS TO ALIGN YOUR WHOLE LIFE TO A DEFINED SET OF VALUES, THAT WHEN LIVED OUT BENEFIT THE CAUSE TO WHICH YOU HAVE ALIGNED YOURSELF.

When we examine Jesus' life and look at His behaviours, we see His beliefs emerge, from which we can discern His values. For example, Jesus hated sin, and sought ways to navigate through the complexity of human sin by seeking out and holding onto grace – grace that was to epitomise His offering to humanity.

An occurrence that springs to mind was the woman who was caught in adultery and dragged before Jesus as a test. In John 8 we find Jesus teaching those who were gathered in the temple courts. It was early morning and Jesus, using His whiteboard skills on the sand, drew with a stick to illustrate His point, when all of a sudden the peaceful morning was shattered. The Pharisees had found a woman, caught in bed with a man she was not married to. They had illegally released the man and now sought to use this woman to test Jesus, as this grace He had been speaking of was unstomachable to them. 'Teacher, this woman was caught in the act of adultery. In the Law Moses commanded us to stone such women. Now what do you say?' (Jn 8:4–5)

Let's hit the pause button, step back and ask a question: what does Jesus value? The answer helps us understand what was happening. Jesus valued those who were oppressed – the poor, the sick, the outcast, the foolish, the sinner. He loved them in a way that wasn't quaint lip service, but was a devotion to them that the culture was not accustomed to. He valued the law, expressing previously that His desire was not to abolish, dismiss or override the law but to show people what the law was meant to achieve – reconciliation with God (Mt 5:17). We also know that He valued the Pharisees. He always respected them and the position they occupied. This didn't stop Him from arguing with them, but it was evident that He valued the platform upon which they stood. The other thing Jesus valued was a hatred for sin. Not the person who sinned but the sin itself. All of these values sat within and complemented His vision.

If Jesus' vision was to see His Kingdom advance into all of creation bringing freedom and transformation to all people, then any value that didn't necessitate this vision would have put the brakes on the influence He had been given. Values do that; they slow down our influence if we do not align them with the Cause. We all know this. You know it when you sit under a leader and they do something more than once that causes you to question their integrity, love or motives. Because of their lack of self-awareness when it comes to their values, they might tell a lie that you know is a lie, or say something about someone in a way that jars you, or reveal a little breach in their integrity. You don't stop following them straightaway, but you are now cautious, trust them less, and this reduces their ability to influence you. You are not so eager to chase them into battle, or stand with them.

In Jesus there was no contradiction or gap. We see this in how He responds, without violating any of His values, while simultaneously fulfilling His vision. We read, 'But Jesus bent down and started to write on the ground with His finger. When they kept on questioning Him, He straightened up and said to them ...' Jesus refuses to be pressured by other's time frames – another value we see that defines His leadership – and then He stands and speaks. 'Let any one of you who is without sin be the first to throw a stone at her.' (Jn 8:7) This is a brilliant bringing together of His values and vision. He is not willing to stand for the sin of omission that the Pharisees committed that led them to this point – that is, to punish the woman when the absence of the male was so clear. The Pharisees are each convicted and leave, the wisest first. Jesus, however, is not finished. When the Pharisees depart and His original class remains, now with the woman standing before Him, Jesus says '... neither do I condemn you, Go now and leave your life of sin.' (Jn 8:11) His love freed this woman of the persecution the Pharisees wanted to bring upon her, but His love also refused to let her stay captive to her sin. Grace abounds from the lips of Jesus and infiltrates those who engage with Him.

As we read the Gospel narratives, it becomes apparent what Jesus values and that He knew and lived out these values. They determined His behaviour.

THE ANONYMOUS LEADER REALISES THEIR BEHAVIOURS MUST ALIGN WITH THEIR VALUES. THEIR VALUES ARE A FENCE GUIDING THEM TO USE THEIR INFLUENCE TO MOVE PEOPLE TOWARD THE CAUSE.

Identifying your values

To identify what your values are, answer the following questions about what you believe:

- Who are you?
- How should people be led?
- Who is God?
- What is God able to achieve?
- Why is your Cause important to you?

Now take your list of answers and ask your closest and most trusted friend – it may be your spouse or partner, or perhaps even a mentor – if they would agree with your self-perceptions based on what they see in your life. This can be tough, because it's real. Ask them to be honest and help you discover areas you may have missed, misinterpreted about yourself or overlooked. In other words, this should be a discussion not a quick approval process. If you get the latter, ask someone else to help.

In case you were wondering (and in the essence of vulnerability) here are some of my answers to the questions on the list:

- Every person matters to God.
- People will have a fuller experience of life with Jesus in the centre of it.
- Every strategic leadership problem can be solved if the right people are around the table.
- Every person has something of worth to contribute.
- There is good inside everyone and it is my responsibility to call out and celebrate that good.
- The local church is the hope of the world.
- Discipline is worth the trade-off.
- We can push ourselves more than we usually do (we all have untapped potential).

- Nothing is more glorious than God transforming a life.
- Learning should be a lifelong journey.
- Obeying God is the most important thing I can do with my life.
- No-one can out-sin God's grace.
- Creating a vacuum is the best way to call out a leader.

After you have developed your list, start to group ideas together, categorising them under headings. In so doing, you will see a set of values clarify, which will become one of your fences.

Once you've done all the hard work, it's time to ensure that your behaviours align with your values. If a discrepancy exists, something important needs addressing. Analyse your behaviours and evaluate them against your values. Have you said or done things that contradict them? Instead of doing what we often do and excusing these things away, put them front and centre and interrogate the *why* behind them. Knowing why you do what you do gives you a front row seat to your value base.

Vision and values are two essential fences every leader's platform needs. They are not the only ones, though – culture is just as important.

Culture

If the first fence that gives us freedom to lead on the platform is vision and the second is values, the third is culture.

MANAGEMENT GURU PETER DRUCKER SAID, 'CULTURE EATS STRATEGY FOR BREAKFAST.' CULTURE, IN FACT, IS SUCH A HUNGRY BEAST IT DEVOURS EVERYTHING THAT STANDS IN ITS WAY – THE ONE EXCEPTION BEING AN INTENTIONAL LEADER DESIRING IT TO CHANGE.

Everyone knows what culture is even if they cannot fully articulate it. So when I have the opportunity to teach on culture, I ask people to first define it. Over the years I have been surprised and enriched by the offerings people have brought. Here are a few of those definitions:

- The habits of the society.
- The collective expectations of a group of people.
- That invisible force that impacts and determines your interactions.
- The informant to how we feel.
- The appearance of values at work.
- An organisation's subconscious.

That last one captures so much for me.

CULTURE CANNOT BE SEEN, BUT EVERYONE IS AWARE OF IT. IT DETERMINES SO MUCH BUT IS COMPLETELY PASSIVE. IT CAN BE YOUR GREATEST FRIEND OR YOUR MOST GRUESOME ENEMY. PEOPLE WILL DECIDE ON VISION AND VALUES AS A RESULT OF EXPERIENCING YOUR CULTURE. IT IS THE MOST IMPORTANT YET INVISIBLE FORCE IN AN ORGANISATION.

Just like every church, ministry, organisation, business or group has a culture, so does the Kingdom of God. The Kingdom's culture enables us to see what life lived on the platform should look like. Jesus offers us numerous glimpses of Kingdom culture, including the first words of His sermon on the mount: 'Now when Jesus saw the crowds, He went up on a mountainside and sat down. His disciples came to Him, and He began to teach them.'

The eight sentences which followed (Mt 5:3–10) were designed to throw those listening off balance about what His Kingdom was all about. In his book *Sermon on the Mount*, DA Carson gives a wonderful insight into these verses, which I have applied below. We could spend days exploring the intricacies of these beatitudes but there is a Kingdom culture that emerges from these sayings that we need to grasp.

When Jesus said, 'Blessed are the poor in spirit, for theirs is the Kingdom of Heaven', He is using an Old Testament root word that ties 'poor' to humble. Those who worshipped God were known as 'poor in spirit' or 'humble in spirit' because they recognised their need for God. Kingdom culture is about God leading the leader first, so the leader might offer that leadership to her people.

When Jesus said, 'Blessed are those who mourn, for they will be comforted', He was exposing the heart of the Kingdom. All believers should feel a grief when they consider all that sin has taken away. Sin should shock us by the horrific offence it is to God – both the sin we commit and the sins that steal others from God. The comforting is in the grace – not a warm grandmother-like cuddle, but the power God has claimed over sin. Sin will not have the last word – a thought that should comfort us. Kingdom culture is about God offering grace to disempower sin, through the lives of those who love Him.

When Jesus said, 'Blessed are the meek, for they will inherit the earth', He was speaking of discipline, resilience and security. DA Carson says, 'Meekness is a controlled desire to see other's interests advance ahead of one's own.' This perspective on life allows a person to let go of all they might otherwise strive to hold onto.

AN ANONYMOUS LEADER IS A MEEK LEADER.

The inheritance spoken of is reminiscent of God's promise to the Israelites that they will have home, security and land to call their own. Kingdom culture is about God's generosity taking care of anyone who prefers everyone else.

When Jesus said, 'Blessed are those who hunger and thirst for righteousness, for they will be filled', He was calling to those who realised they could not continue to live without righteousness – that is, being right with God. In hungering and thirsting for such things, a person yearns to conform to God's will. In so doing, their famished soul is met by God's willingness to fill them. Kingdom culture is about God's will completely defining a person to the point of utter dependence on God.

When Jesus said, 'Blessed are the merciful, for they will be shown mercy', He was wanting those who had much to reach out to those who had less – those on the margins, who were hated by society or lonely, and meet them with compassion and kindness. In saying this, Jesus wants His hearers to see how undeserving they too are of God's mercy. Through this understanding, they are able to both give and receive mercy. Kingdom culture is about God's compassion and kindness becoming the first action we take. We are empowered because of God's initiated action toward us already.

When Jesus said, 'Blessed are the pure in heart, for they will see God', He was wanting to impress upon all of His listeners that a pure heart was the most essential and indispensable prerequisite for relating to God. Purity is so important because the Kingdom of God is a pure Kingdom, led by a holy and pure King. It is only through purity defining our hearts that we will consistently encounter God.

When Jesus said, 'Blessed are the peacemakers, for they will be called children of God', He was calling them to walk in His footsteps, both physical and spiritual. Jesus was the epitome of peacemaking – not peacekeeping – first and foremost by creating peace between us and God. Our peacemaking is to permeate into every aspect of our lives, words and actions. In living as such, we become children (or in some versions, sons) of God. This is not a gendered term but refers to the culturally relevant dynamic of the development of the Father's character in His offspring. As peace increases in our souls, so does the character of God in our lives. Kingdom culture is about God's character defining all that we are.

When Jesus said, 'Blessed are those who are persecuted because of righteousness, for theirs is the Kingdom of Heaven.' To be defined by righteousness was to be determined to live as God wills a person to live. This will bring opposition as it works itself out in a person's life, because it is the righteousness in a person's life that causes social, political and religious friction, as the things of God are embodied and come to affect the things of this world. Kingdom culture is about God's righteousness affecting the state of this world through the lives of those who follow.

Finding your culture

One of the four fences of the Anonymous Leader's platform is culture. The Anonymous Leader has to lead in such a way that he embraces and lives out that culture, never violating, challenging or crossing it.

Kingdom culture requires the Anonymous Leader to:

- Take his lead from God.
- Prefer everyone else whom she leads.
- Depend on God's providence as he leads.
- Always treat others with kindness and compassion.
- Cultivate a pure heart.
- Always be developing and exhibiting the character of Christ.
- Lead righteously, so that the desires of God come to define a new reality.

A very poignant question which helps a leader begin to identify what the culture fence looks like, especially in relation to where they are situated, is this: what is the culture of your heart?

This question requires more than ten minutes of contemplation; it requires you to deeply examine the condition of your heart. Your answers will reveal any discrepancies between your heart's culture and God's Kingdom culture. Addressing these differences will give you more freedom and opportunity to influence others from your platform.

Vision, values and culture are three of the four fences which offer guidance and clarity to a leader. The final one is a leader's heart or motive, which can be at times overlooked – but to do so is at a leader's peril.

Heart

If a leader compromises the vision they are calling others to, they move away from the platform of God's influence. If a leader violates the values of the Kingdom of God, then something of God's influence is diluted and lost. If a leader does not honour Kingdom culture, they can fulfil the vision and even complement the values, but they cannot continue to influence others for the benefit and glory of God.

As I thought about these three platform fences, I deliberated on what the fourth might be. What is essential to lead people like Jesus led them? To enable God's influence to move them forward? What, if it were absent, would prevent these things from taking place? I came to the conclusion (having to leave some strong candidates behind) that the answer was heart, or motive.

THE CONDITION OF OUR HEARTS DETERMINES THE REASONS FOR OUR ACTIONS. IF WE HAVE A BITTER HEART, WE WILL ACT OUT OF REVENGE

OR MALICE. IF YOUR HEART IS INFUSED WITH JOY, YOU WILL ACT WITH GENEROSITY AND GRACE. OUR HEART DETERMINES THE MANNER OF OUR ENGAGEMENT AND THAT IS CALLED A MOTIVE – THE REASON WE DO WHAT WE DO.

Motives are the *why* behind all that we do. They are what shape, drive and flavour everything. If a leader has a job that needs doing, the manner in which he approaches and asks someone for help with that job reveals his motives. A leader may use force and demand someone do the job, revealing a selfish motive: 'I need this job done; you will do it.' A leader may use manipulation to drag someone into the task, either by guilt, reward or pity, revealing again a selfish motive.

THE ANONYMOUS LEADER, HOWEVER, WANTS THE JOB FILLED BECAUSE OF THE OPPORTUNITIES IT PRESENTS TO THE ONE WHO MIGHT FILL IT. THEY SEEK THE RIGHT PERSON OUT, KNOWING IF THAT PERSON CHOOSES TO HELP, THEY WILL BE BLESSED IN DOING SO.

For the Anonymous Leader, force or manipulation are the furthest things from their intentions. Instead, the leader casts a compelling and exciting vision to captivate this person with the Cause. The Anonymous Leader realises it is not at all about them, but about the Cause.

On a side note, people stay in roles far longer if they are 'vision cast' into them, rather than muscled or manipulated in; they also enjoy them longer and like you more. All these aspects are a product of the leader's motives.

In what is thought to be the first Christian hymn, featured by Paul in his letter to the Church of Philippi, he reveals the motives behind Christ's ministry. It begins with Paul's introduction: 'In your relationships with one another, have the same mindset as Christ Jesus'. (Phil 2:5) I love that Jesus set His mind not just to the task ahead, but also to how He was going to do it – that He would engage from a certain approach which would ensure He occupied the correct platform.

Paul goes on, 'Who, being in very nature God, did not consider equality with God something to be used to his own advantage; rather, he made himself nothing by taking the very nature of a servant, being made in human likeness.' (Phil 2:6–7) Jesus considered Himself carefully and accurately, realising He was God, but wanting to reveal to us what human leadership needed to look like. He put aside that which would have expanded His influence, His Godliness, so that through His human ministry, the influence that was present belonged to God.

Jesus saw no value in forcing people to follow Him; instead He chose to win them to Him. In order to do that, He put aside His equality with God and became nothing, ensuring that all He did would authentically serve and love people. Jesus eradicated from His leadership, before He began, any opportunity for pride, arrogance or shortcuts that might get in the way. He ensured His motives were held to the ideal of servanthood and love.

'... being found in appearance as a man, he Humbled himself by becoming obedient to death – even death on a cross!' (Phil 2:8) If ever His motives were to be tested, it was on the cross. Crucifixion peeled back the layers of a man so that all that was true about them was on show for everyone to see. The cross reveals the condition of Christ's heart.

When Jesus endured the cross, we hear him saying sentences like, 'Father, forgive them, for they do not know what they are doing.' (Lk 23:34) or 'Truly I tell you, today you will be with me in paradise.' (Lk 23:43) or 'Father, into your hands I commit my spirit.' (Lk 23:46)

Throughout the most excruciating method of death the Romans had, Jesus' motives rang true to all He had said and done. He was doing all of it for humankind, His heart was motivated by a purity of love, creation had not yet seen. Even in His words, 'My God, my God, why have you forsaken me?' (Mt 27:46), we see His heart was relational. He quotes the 22nd Psalm, a Psalm of David that captures the desolation of the circumstance He was enduring. These words both express the cry of His heart, while enabling us to relate to Him with the struggles of our own situations. Jesus' heart was to give all for the Cause, regardless of the cost and, in so doing, provide us with hope when we feel the same.

'Therefore God exalted Him to the highest place and gave him the name that is above every name, that at the name of Jesus every knee should bow, in heaven and on earth and under the earth, and every tongue acknowledge that Jesus Christ is Lord, to the glory of God the Father.' (Phil 2:5–11) Jesus' motive to decrease so that God could increase – His decision to become less so that God would become more – results in Jesus' impact being all about the influence of God. This left Jesus in the hands of God, for God to do what He wished with Him. God consequently exalted Christ as King, and we see the beautiful path Anonymous Leadership takes.

THE ANONYMOUS LEADER NEEDN'T WORRY ABOUT THEIR FUTURE, IF THEIR PRESENT BELONGS TO GOD. THEIR PRESENT BELONGS TO GOD AS THEIR MIND BECOMES SET ON THAT. WHEN A PERSON'S MIND IS SET ON A PARTICULAR ORIENTATION, THEIR HEART FOLLOWS THE SAME COURSE AND THEIR MOTIVES BECOME SECURE IN THAT DIRECTION. ANONYMOUS LEADERSHIP IS ABOUT LEADING WITH THE MOTIVES, THE HEART OF CHRIST.

Developing your heart

Some questions that may help explore this further are:

- Is what I am doing wholly for the sake of the Cause to which I have given my life?
- Can I gain from this in any way?
- What is the *why* that informs my decision-making?
- Would someone be inspired if they could see all the inner convictions I apply to my decision-making process?
- Do I want what is best for others and for the church, even if it costs me?

These are challenging questions, but they are necessary if we are to lead with pure motives and not cross a fence line.

In chapter 7, we explore how we can define the platform's fences for the leaders we lead, and how this impacts the way they lead.

7

FENCING IN THE PLATFORM FOR LEADERS AND TEAMS

LEADING LEADERS IS not easy, and leading emerging leaders is even tougher.

A while back there was a leader who I'd identified, empowered and released but who wasn't reaching his leadership potential, seeming to be lazy, distracted and unmotivated. I'd heard enough complaints to know there were problems, and as his absence increased, his reliability decreased. Trust was disappearing and I should have spoken to him weeks earlier. Finally I asked to meet. I was disappointed in him and myself.

The moments before these meetings are always worse in our heads than they are in real life. As we began to talk, what became clear were not the failings of this emerging leader, but my failing as his leader. I had lacked one of the essential elements any follower requires: clarity.

I had not been clear about what I wanted him to do – it was clear in my head, but not in my communication.

He said to me, 'I've been trying to do what you asked, but I'm not sure exactly what it is that you want me to do.' I retorted by repeating my earlier instructions and then asked, 'So when I said that, it wasn't clear enough for you?'

To which he responded with, 'No, not really. Did you want me to do it like this ... or like that ... What sort of result were you after? I could have done this ... but then I wasn't sure if in fact you wanted things to look like that ...' It was a productive conversation, and I shouldn't have been anxious about it.

I had not provided him with the fences that would have guided his efforts. I'd told him to run in a vague direction, thinking I was giving him freedom to succeed. I had not given him freedom; I had disempowered him and as a result he had charged through more than one fence.

EVERY LEADER NEEDS TO KNOW WHAT THE FENCES OF THE PLATFORM LOOK LIKE SO THEY CAN FOCUS ON ACHIEVING THE TASK THEY ARE SET.

One-line platform descriptions

Andy Stanley first introduced me to the concept of one-line job descriptions – where one sentence captures the entire job description. This makes the job expectations easy to remember and provides clarity and focus.

An example of a one-line job description might be:

- Create environments where people can explore faith.
- Increase people's awareness of the presence of God in corporate worship.
- Raise publicity and funds for our mission partners.

- Disciple young people so they're equipped to disciple their friends.
- Develop leaders who develop leaders.

Creating a one-line job description was the first step I took in offering greater guidance to the emerging leader I was working with.

This type of job description clarifies the purposes that our platform has, for a season of ministry. Clarity is then also required in designing the fences for the platform.

The platform model works on both a macro and micro level. It helps us frame and explore the call of God on the whole of our lives, while also empowering us to empower those we lead.

Sitting with this emerging leader, I drew him the diagram on page 91. The rectangle represents the platform we have as leaders. Everything we do needs to happen inside the fenced-in platform. Each platform has four fences (vision, values, culture and heart – refer to chapter 6).

WHEN INVITING PEOPLE INTO NEW ROLES, WE NEED TO DEFINE THE FENCES OF THE PLATFORM FOR THEM. THESE FENCES DEMAND OUR RESPECT AND MUST NEVER BE CROSSED, BUT IT'S UNFAIR TO ASSUME NEW LEADERS WILL NATURALLY KNOW WHAT THESE FENCES ARE WITHOUT BEING TOLD.

Highlighting in meticulous detail what is required of a leader may feel like a costly exercise, but it is actually a great investment. Emerging leaders need the opportunity to learn as they go, which they can only have if they lead from an informed position. If we assume they know what we know, we disservice their growth.

As we explored in chapter 6, this framework enables clarity. We position a leader to lead well when we let them know what is expected of them, create clear vision for them to pursue, nurture their spirit of service, and identify the culture that needs strengthening. Doing this enabled the conversation I had with the emerging leader (at the beginning of this chapter) to lead to wonderful outcomes that benefited many.

The edges your platform needs

Leadership always occurs in the context of people – in most cases, in a team setting. In chapter 6 we explored how the platform's fences relate to your personal leadership, but it is also important that we explore how the fences of the platform influence ministry done in a team. Understanding this will equip you to lead with greater effectiveness.

In the following sections, I again outline the four fences of the leadership platform, this time relating to team settings.

Vision

In the very first ministry I ran, our vision was simple: to lead people to Jesus Christ. This vision captured what we wanted to achieve, and everything we did was about pursuing this vision. We wanted each leader to lead the people in their care to Jesus Christ. It was a defining fence to their leadership platform.

In every form of ministry, each leader was coached to think, *How do I lead this young person to Jesus?* Whether that be through having a conversation with a person, running a program, developing material or brainstorming initiatives, each leader was to hold the vision front and centre. If a leader began to stray from our vision, realignment would take place. The vision fenced in the platform, and everything the leader did needed to work within and contribute to that vision.

Values

If a ministry has the value of inclusivity – that is, all the people present should be able to participate – then the programs need to be sensitive, for example, to those with a disability or limitation. This creates a boundary around what can and can't be done. If a leader comes up with an idea that limits the engagement of some people, it clashes with the value of inclusivity, meaning the idea is not allowed to happen. The boundaries regulate what happens on the platform.

If a value is hospitality, the ministry needs to do all it can to ensure those attending for the first time are warmly welcomed and assimilated into community. If a person is welcomed with excellence but then left to find their own way, the value of hospitality is compromised and a fence crossed.

VALUES ARE A CLEAR GUIDE FOR THE LEADERS' BEHAVIOUR AND THE ENGAGEMENT THAT OCCURS. EACH LEADER MUST LIVE WITHIN THE VALUES THAT THE TEAM DECIDE.

If a value is compassion and a leader is heard judging a person, the behaviour needs to be named as a violation of the values and of the platform's fence. In this way, the integrity of the platform is preserved because of the strength of its fences.

Culture

One of the unconscious expectations of a team – the culture – might be that a common respect and honour exists between them. This would create safety and belonging, encouraging people to participate. If someone started to dishonour others in the team, the culture would be violated. If this were then tolerated, it would become the culture. Culture is like that: it is swayed by the loudest voice.

THE FENCE ENSURES THAT CULTURE IS UPHELD, AND SO A BREACH OF CULTURE SHOULD NEVER BE TOLERATED. LEADERS NEED TO REALISE WHAT THE CULTURE IS AND HOW JUST ONE TEAM MEMBER'S BEHAVIOUR CAN THREATEN IT.

When a leader joins a team, they need to be clear on what is expected of them culturally. Some questions that facilitate this are:

- How are people treated?
- How are relationships between the team expected to be conducted?
- How do we understand aspects such as power, confidentiality, expectations, grace, theology, systems, standards and relationships?

All of these things and more create the culture of a ministry. If the fence is clearly understood and respected, everyone's experience is enhanced and everyone benefits.

Heart

Heart is the most important fence in ensuring the sustainability of Anonymous Leadership in a team on a God-given platform. The heart with which someone approaches ministry determines the shape and form of their ministry. When a person commences in a leadership role, they will have a mix of motives. Part of their heart wants to serve, love, encourage and bless others, while another part of their heart is drawn to the allure of power, influence and ambition.

Every leader, at least when they begin, has conflicting motives. The confusion comes from an unrealistic expectation of how their experience should be. It is important to sit with an emerging leader and help them identify their motives. Once identified, we can then take the opportunity to be clear on what they can expect – the sacrifice it will take, the opportunity it will provide to partner with God changing lives, and the inevitable heartbreak that awaits them. Having these conversations early in a leader's journey will help them to align their motives as they start to lead people.

Often emerging leaders are determined to follow their heart, making Jeremiah's insights helpful. He said 'The heart is deceitful above all things.' (Jer 17:9) The heart desires and pursues things that wisdom would say *no* to. The same is true in leadership. Often we desire things, which we are not even aware we desire, and we use our leadership to obtain them. Heart surgery and motive alignment is an essential step in any emerging leader's journey, and it is the responsibility of their leader to facilitate it.

KNOWING THE FENCES OF THE PLATFORM IS IMPERATIVE TO OCCUPYING THE PLATFORM. WITHOUT UNDERSTANDING THE EXPECTATIONS, A LEADER IS DESTINED TO CROSS A FENCE THEY WOULD RATHER NOT. BEING CLEAR ABOUT THE VISION, VALUES, CULTURE AND MOTIVES NEEDED FOR EFFECTIVE LEADERSHIP IS VITAL.

If an Anonymous Leader can understand and communicate these things, they are positioned to influence a great many lives for the Cause they are leading.

UNDERSTANDING THE WORK OF THE HOLY SPIRIT

'DO YOU NOT know that your body is a temple of the Holy Spirit, who is in you, whom you have received from God? You are not your own; you were bought at a price. Therefore honour God with your body.' (1 Cor 6:19–20) These words belong to the Apostle Paul, who sought to provoke the members of the Church in Corinth to understand themselves differently. In this passage, Paul finishes his reprimand of their sexual exploitations before moving on to address marriage, which they had asked him about.

In concluding his point Paul offers this revelation, relevant to not only our sexuality, but also our identity. 'Do you not know?' he asks. This understanding should be the most elementary of every Christ follower; the Holy Spirit dwells in us. This means the things we are able to do are the result of God inhabiting our bodies.

THE INFLUENCE WE HAVE IS NOT JUST OUR INFLUENCE BUT GOD'S INFLUENCE, SHAPING AND FORMING THE INFLUENCE WE HAVE.

'Do you not know that your body is a temple of the Holy Spirit?' Paul asserts, but how frequently as leaders do we forget this most foundational truth of faith. This then manifests in a number of ways: we claim the glory for ourselves; we feel accomplished because of what we were able to achieve; we privately recall the results of our genius while conveying to the world that it was God's action. Every leader is guilty of this failing – it's known as being human.

The Holy Spirit's influence

In Scripture, we see that the Spirit of God resides in those who call upon God. With the presence of God's Spirit comes God's influence. The Scriptures, however, appear elusive on what happens when that influence is used for ill-gotten gain. Understanding this dynamic of influence is important as we explore Anonymous Leadership.

Jesus will continue to build His church, sometimes with us and sometimes in spite of us, but we control the permission we give the Holy Spirit to use us in this endeavour. As leaders whose influence is informed by the influence of God, our primary task is to align our will with God's. If our will is aligned with God's will, the purposes and heart of God are developed in our purpose and heart. This enables us to discern God's will and lead complementary to His influence, influencing others to do the same.

The Holy Spirit's influence through us enables us to expand and define our leadership, if we first permit and then surrender to the Holy Spirit. If we refuse to permit or surrender, God's Spirit doesn't leave us or choose not to dwell in us. For God is faithful and redemptive, even towards and within those He asks to lead (Rom 11:29).

God has given Himself to us. He lives in us. He has never been elitist about who He chooses to inhabit. The Scriptures tell us those who recognise Him as their Lord and surrender to Him as Saviour are those whom He inhabits (Jn 1:12; Rom 10:9; 1 Cor 3:16). Sinners now categorised as saints, who then learn to become saints. Once the Holy Spirit comes to live in a person, that same Spirit sets about advancing God's Kingdom through this life now surrendered to God's purposes. This means God is still able to work out His purposes through fallen, broken, self-centred, arrogant, insecure, careless, dishonest, shallow, ambitious or pride-filled leaders.

You can likely easily find articles and reports on leaders who have accomplished much in building the Kingdom of God, only to have a hidden and devastating sin (or sins) uncovered, which have ended their ministry. Exploring the case studies here is of no benefit; instead, it's important to celebrate what God does in spite of human flaws and limitations, and our sins and weaknesses. This is possible because the influence we have is not only our own. The Holy Spirit's work through our leadership is what bears fruit that lasts.

UNBELIEVABLE THINGS CAN HAPPEN AS A PERSON MARRIES THEIR NATURAL GOD-GIVEN INFLUENCE, CHARISMA AND PERSONHOOD WITH THE PERSONHOOD, INFLUENCE AND CHARISMA OF GOD. THE ANONYMOUS LEADER RECOGNISES THAT TO LEAD WITHOUT MARRYING HER INFLUENCE TO GOD'S WOULD BE TO DISHONOUR THE PLATFORM SHE INHABITS.

The Anonymous Leader realises she was born to lead for, and with, God. To do anything else would be a distortion of the image she was created in.

PART II SUMMARY

In the centre of the platform we become anonymous as Christ becomes all that is seen in our leadership. If we move from the centre of the platform, pursuing our ambitions, we find ourselves crossing the fences that are put up to guide our influence. When this happens, we forfeit some and eventually all of our influence. The mature leader understands that they need to steward their passion, trust, invincibility, confidence and commitment toward Christ – surrendering themselves and these components to Christ, that He might redeem them. When these components are not surrendered to Christ but are invested in self-ambition, we see a very different flavour of leadership emerge.

This then provides a helpful test of a leader's inner life. If a leader detects within himself substantial elements of recklessness, hypocrisy, pride, insecurity or shallowness on a consistent basis, he can realise he is leading more out of ambition than anonymity. The danger for such a leader is that the care of others becomes a secondary priority to his own agenda. He will use others to achieve his own ends. He will disregard the Cause of Christ for the sake of his own cause. He will hurt others and discard them when they are no longer valuable – all the while believing that he is in fact leading in a manner God desires.

We all need to be alert to this in our own leadership. We are all susceptible to selfish ambition. This is a tension of leadership, but not one we need to be subdued by. The Anonymous Leader seeks to arrest her drift away from Christ, and strives to move toward the centre of the platform.

Part II summary

The next part of the book will explore the five main components present in every person who is ever asked to lead. These components develop as a person leads – and what they develop into is up to the leader. These components can develop into Christlike qualities that enable the influence of God to flourish in a leader's life, or they can develop into self-ambitious qualities that usher a leader from the platform – ultimately, forfeiting their influence. This happens when we move beyond the borders of the platform.

Just past the fences of the platform are the borders. Think of a platform's borders like you think about the land between a farmer's fence and the edge of their property. While the fences are there to keep the cows in, they do not always signify the end of the farmer's property, especially when the land meets a road. The borders represent the edge of the farmer's property. Grasping this is crucial to understanding the chapters in part III.

A further analogy is the border of a country. In the last few years, I have had the privilege of leading various mission teams into Cambodia to work with our mission partner in the city of Poipet. To reach Poipet, you must fly into Bangkok and drive five hours down to the Thai–Cambodian border. Once at the border, you show your papers and move through passport control, thinking you're about to enter Cambodia. This is, however, not the case.

Instead, you find yourself in 'no-man's-land'. This is a strip of land that lies between Thailand and Cambodia, about a kilometre wide, which you need to cross in order to enter either country. On that land, casinos, restaurants, markets and all kinds of other infrastructure have been developed. If you are a Thai national, you can enter no-man's-land without a passport and do what you like there. If you are Cambodian, the same rules apply. This means Thai and Cambodian people can trade whatever they like and not be searched because they are not leaving their own country. It is no wonder this border is the most highly trafficked border in the world.

Where the actual border marker lies can be murky, but both the Thai and Cambodian people are clear on when they have completely left their own land. The same can be said of the Anonymous Leader's platform. The borders to the platform are not clear, unlike the fences. Where the borders start and finish can be a bit murky, but for a leader there does come a point of clarity – when you know you have vacated the platform and crossed beyond a border.

The Anonymous Leader doesn't concern himself with where the border of the platform finishes. His calling is to occupy the centre of the platform. Jesus lived His entire life in the centre of the platform. He was the complete culmination of wisdom, integrity, resilience, humility and security. As we explore the five foundational leadership components – passion, trust, invincibility, confidence and commitment – we have the responsibility and opportunity to steward them toward the Christlike template of leadership.

PART III

THE FIVE FOUNDATIONAL LEADERSHIP COMPONENTS

9

MIGRATING PASSION INTO WISDOM

WE WERE SITTING in the old church hall, on a Tuesday night, a week before I was to start as the new minister. I had been looking forward to this for more than three years. I had just turned 25, and thought I knew a lot more than I did. The elders and I were meeting to discuss the vision of the church. They were both excited and apprehensive, and who could blame them?

Leading up to the meeting, I had spent time preparing for both that gathering and my ministry there. I didn't want to overwhelm these unsuspecting elders, but at the same time I saw this was a valuable opportunity to reveal some of the hopes and dreams I had.

We sat in a circle, slowly working through the agenda, when I asked, 'Could I share some things that I've been thinking about?' I then launched into a passionate vision cast that must have seemed quite out of place. I remember their faces – some sparked with enthusiasm and wonder, others seemed to eye me with benign suspicion, and one stared as though in shock. Looking back it was a beautiful moment that taught me so much. After I had monopolised the airwaves for quite a while, the elder who was clearly shocked spoke up and said, 'You do realise we need to go slowly, don't you?'

THAT'S THE THING ABOUT PASSION – IT DOESN'T UNDERSTAND SPEED. IT EXPECTS EVERYTHING TO HAPPEN RIGHT NOW, BECAUSE TIME IS OF THE ESSENCE. IT DRIVES US OUT OF BED AND INTO THE SPACE GOD HAS CALLED US. IT STIRS SO DEEPLY IN OUR EMOTIONS THAT SLEEP CAN BE HARD TO COME BY. IT REDEFINES THINGS WITH HOPE AND POSSIBILITY, AND FUELS US TO DO THAT WHICH WE MIGHT NORMALLY TURN AWAY FROM.

Every emerging leader is passionate – indeed, it's one of the core components of everyone who leads. Regardless of their competence, character and experience, everyone who raises their hand to lead and steps onto the platform of leadership does so because they are passionate to make a difference for someone, somewhere, somehow. The recognition of passion precedes the recognition of leadership. Not everyone with a passion is a leader, but everyone who is a leader is passionate.

Passion enables a leader to achieve what might seem impossible to others, depending on its increase or decrease in maturity. Passion is not a static characteristic, but is influenced by multiple factors that a leader encounters as they lead. These factors include the presence or absence of:

- vision
- encouragement and/or discouragement
- challenging circumstances faced
- support
- reactions to hardship.

Every emerging leader has the choice to direct their passion toward anonymity or self-ambition. The direction you point your passion in determines what your leadership looks like.

When that elder said, 'You do realise we need to go slowly, don't you?' I wanted to say the first thing that came to my mind: 'I really need you all to be with me on this journey; otherwise, it's not going to be much fun at all. We have an opportunity to achieve great things but time is of the essence. There's not a minute to lose.' But what I said was, 'Of course! It's not like we're going to do all these things next week.' Which was true – to do all I wanted in one week would have been very impressive; I'd given myself at least a month.

Passion automatically wants to move very fast. It is a catalyst for action and requires those with it to speed up what they are doing in order to effect change.

Harnessing your passion

Passion harnessed has so much more potential and power, because it is informed – by the current culture, climate and position of those it will affect. It is informed by the story that has preceded that time, which harbours hurts, disappointments, victories and joys. It is informed by the current resources and capacity available to step into the future – including the available energy, finance, people and, of course, corporate discernment of where God is leading. All these things, when informing passion, produce wisdom. Wisdom, to flourish, requires passion to slow down but not dilute. The wise words of that elder didn't squash or dilute my passion; they focused and informed it.

Every emerging leader is passionate, but their passion is often untamed or unharnessed. That passion will either move toward anonymity or self-ambition and the road to anonymity is laden with sandpaper – sandpaper that doesn't remove, take away or wear down a leader's passion, but shapes, qualifies, directs and informs it.

Emerging leaders encounter sandpaper moments when:

- They speak with a mentor who asks them tough questions that slow them down.
- They suggest an exciting idea that is dismissed because of the unwise risk.
- They are reprimanded for unchecked behaviour.
- They face a disappointment or failure, which significantly challenges them.

All of these scenarios (and more) gradually mould a leader's passion into wisdom.

As a leader's passion undergoes the sandpapering process, they surrender more and more to the Cause for which they want to lead. This happens through criticism, triumphs, disappointments, wins, frustrations and celebrations – all of which inform a leader's passion. Ministry is a natural smoothing agent, refining a leader's passion, something that is absolutely necessary as the leader is transformed from a passionate leader into a wise and passionate leader.

INFORMING EXPERIENCES SHOULD NEVER COMPLETELY DETERMINE A LEADER'S PASSION. ON THE CONTRARY, EVERY ELEMENT THAT INFORMS PASSION IS A CONVERSATION PARTNER WHOSE VOICE NEEDS TO BE DISCERNED, BUT NOT ALL OF THESE CONVERSATION PARTNERS NEED TO BE LISTENED TO.

What are you focusing your passion on?

After five wonderful years, I moved from my first church placement to take on the role of youth and young adults pastor at Newlife (a larger church, as I've mentioned earlier). The main objective of my role was to grow the Youth Ministry and establish a Young Adults Ministry.

Three months after establishing the Young Adults Ministry, Lyndal and I found ourselves in a conversation with the 25 young adults who called Newlife home. I recall the meeting as though it were yesterday. The evening service we'd just launched was growing in attendance, and we found ourselves navigating uncharted territory.

Some issues had emerged, and I was keen to identify what they were. Initially I thought the main problem was the music – no-one seemed to be happy with it. Complaints ranged from the music being too slow, fast, loud, soft, acoustic and/or heavy. People were frustrated with the song choice, not engaging with the singing, or upset because there were too many new songs. It was depressingly impressive from only 25 young adults.

As they shared, I listened for what was really being said. Everyone's focus had deteriorated to the music. God, whom we use music to worship, appeared to be absent from the opinions shared.

'Do you think God cares about the music?' I interjected. Holding everyone's attention, I challenged them on why we use music in church. I asked them what had become of our worshipping hearts – which Paul speaks of in Romans 12:1: 'Therefore, I urge you, brothers and sisters, in view of God's mercy, to offer your bodies as a living sacrifice, holy and pleasing to God – this is your true and proper worship.' We sat around that circle, a group of spiritual consumers, getting fat on the pleasures of our culture.

'Perhaps we could cut the music altogether?' I suggested. The silence was deafening, followed by a torrent of questions. 'How would you do it?' 'How long would you do it for? Forever, or for a week?' 'What would others think of it?' 'Would it really be church if we did that?'

I wasn't concerned by the implications the questions raised, I was concerned by our lack of dependence on God and hunger for His presence – whether we were at church on a Sunday or serving our next-door neighbour during the week. We had lost the value of God's transcendent grace because we'd become so caught up in the music. Music had become an end in itself, not a means to an end – to honour and glorify God.

We talked long into the night, agreed and prayed. The following Sunday, there was no music. We didn't sing or play a note; we didn't use live music in the service at all. The week after was the same, as was the one after that. We continued until it became clear that music was to serve our worship, not become it.

I recall the conversations during that period. We discussed the wisdom of the decision, the danger it posed to our outreach potential, and the value it took away from our musicians and singers. Many times, I felt my passion begin to buckle under the weight of public opinion. I remained adamant, however, that when we gathered to worship, it had to be about encountering God and not about genres, volume or style of music.

WE CAN RESENT PEOPLE PUSHING BACK ON OUR PASSION: DON'T, AS THERE IS GREAT WORTH IN IT.

Those words and counterviews honed and informed my passion. As challenging as they were, they affirmed in me the decision we had made. Any reservations expressed should chiefly serve to make us aware of the potential pitfalls and how we might negotiate them.

Because of the sandpaper, I was able to passionately push forward with the idea, while ensuring it was informed, so the decision and its execution would be a wise one.

I held tight to my passionate belief that God was walking us through this season and doing a great work in our spirits. It was six Sundays later when we sang our first song, and a month after that before we were back to a full musical complement. In that time, something had radically shifted in our midst. Something that could not be achieved any other way.

It would have been so easy to allow my insecurities and fears to sabotage my passion and determine what should be done. If that had been so, those same insecurities and fears would have shaped our community, and it would not be today the rich, eclectic mix of young adults it is.

FEAR ROBS PASSION OF ITS INTENSITY. THERE WILL ALWAYS BE AN ADVERSARY TO PASSIONATE FAITH, BUT THAT ADVERSARY DOES NOT NEED TO BE GIVEN ANYTHING. HOLD TO YOUR PASSION, ENSURE IT IS INFORMED BY EVERYTHING AROUND YOU, AND IT WILL GIVE BIRTH TO WISDOM.

The energy of wisdom

A few years ago, a friend of mine asked me a very confronting and challenging question. He said, 'When I look at you I sense that you are not as passionate now as you were when you first started out in ministry. I don't want to end up like that; can you help me understand where you lost your passion and how I might avoid it?'

It bothered me that I couldn't immediately answer the question. But then I realised that his question's assumption was incorrect – I couldn't answer it because I am more passionate now than I was when I started student leading, or discussed my vision with the elders in that church hall, or dreamt with friends about a church with no music. Back then I would have told you that I would give my life for the Cause of Christ; now, you can see that I have.

When you first start leading, you need to convince everyone how passionate you are, and you do this through your attitude, service, sacrifice and engagement. This is necessary to do because you have no other evidence to convince others to follow you. So you lead enthusiastically, inspiring and encouraging people to follow you because of the new ideas you have.

THE LONGER YOU LEAD THE LESS ENERGY YOU FOCUS ON PASSION AND THE MORE YOU FOCUS ON WISDOM. IF YOU ARE PASSIONATE, AFTER LEADING FOR SOME TIME, PEOPLE RECOGNISE YOUR PASSION IN THE WAY YOU LEAD AND THE DECISIONS YOU MAKE. THEY MAY CONFUSE IT SOMETIMES FOR WISDOM AND SAY YOU'RE WISE MORE THAN YOU ARE PASSIONATE, BUT WISDOM IS PASSION INFORMED AND INTENSIFIED.

I don't have the need, and nor do those who choose to follow me, to rush around with inexhaustible, extroverted, excited energy. I once did, but now I lead differently. Those who follow me just need to know that I have laid my life down for the Cause, well before I've invited them to do the same.

Allowing your wisdom to become self-evident

A couple of years ago we commenced a capital campaign at Newlife to raise $6 million. This would enable us to develop our property, build a 1000-seat auditorium, and create greater opportunities for ministry and mission. When it came time to vision cast for finances, I sat in a precarious situation. At the time, our Young Adult service was attracting around 135 young adults each week. The current auditorium already sat 400 people so, on first analysis, we didn't need an extra 600 seats. How do you invite a group of 20-somethings to sacrificially give each week to a need that they can see is not relevant to them?

What I came to learn was the Anonymous Leader recognises that the Cause is greater than the small part they play in it. After praying about it, I arrived at some conclusions that helped us navigate forward:

- First, our young adults weren't separate from Newlife – we were Newlife, so a vision that was Newlife's, was our vision.

- Second, we weren't going to remain at 135 young adults each week if God continued to do what He was already doing.

- Third, we had the chance to sew into the spiritual future of those who had never come to church, did not yet know Christ and who would be sitting next to us in the years to come.

- Fourth, why should we restrict our vision to people who are the same as us? We needed to be passionately investing in people of all ages.

I was passionate about this – about seeing people who didn't know Jesus trust Him with their lives, put their faith in Him and become part of His transformative and redeeming movement, called the Church.

This vision gripped Lyndal and I and we welcomed the opportunity to give to it, which we did. We told people what the vision was and invited them to join us. Then we told them we had given to it sacrificially, and we invited them to give. The profound generosity which then flowed from our young adults and into this project was overwhelming.

I no longer have to work to convince people I am passionate. They see it in the vision I cast, the commitment I model and the decisions I make, which all flow out of wisdom. Wisdom is passion, only slowed down and informed.

When passion turns toward recklessness

They accompanied Jesus their leader to Gethsemane Garden, where He had gone to pray. He instructed them to stand guard while He went further into the garden. It was too late in the day, however – too much had happened and the call of sleep was too strong. Peter, James and John all succumbed to the temptation – and not just once but twice. And they would have succumbed a third time if Jesus had not woken them the second time He returned. All of a sudden Jesus was there, summoning His weary followers: 'Rise, let us go! Here comes my betrayer.'(Mt 26:46)

Out of the darkness appeared Judas, one of their own. He sidled up to Jesus, kissing him and unleashing hell. Suddenly soldiers were everywhere, torches were waved, swords drawn and voices raised. That's when it happened. Peter couldn't control himself – he was a passionate man who lived on the edge. He would often act before he thought; his body or mouth always pre-empting his mind. His compatriots knew this, which is likely why Matthew and Luke chose not to mention it was Peter. (Again!)

John, however, wasn't as considerate, telling us, 'Then Simon Peter, who had a sword, drew it and struck the high priest's servant, cutting off his right ear.' (Jn 18:10) That Peter was wearing a sword that night indicated his passionate resolve to defend his leader, but he was reckless. When passion is unchecked or misinformed, it results in reckless behaviour. He unsheathed his weapon, swung blindly and hit poor Malchus – who was in the fray, but hardly someone to blame. Peter unleashed his passion and cut a man's ear off. He was passionate about defending and protecting Jesus, about responding to injustice and making sure others knew exactly where he stood. His passion was good but it was determined by his self-ambition.

Previously, Jesus had told the disciples what was to happen, and how it would take place. He even informed Peter of his betrayal after Jesus was arrested. Peter had disagreed, assuring Jesus this would not happen. Peter had faith in himself – he knew what needed to be done and what would happen, even if Jesus didn't. This, of course, is what passion produces – a focused mindset. As we read the story, we can see Jesus gradually unfolding His redemptive plan. At the same time, we can see Peter's passion, and the point at which Peter makes the decision that his plan – his way and his agenda – was more viable than Jesus'. Self-ambition does this. We forsake the Cause we have given ourselves to and instead force things to accommodate the plans we have.

It's harder to identify this in our own leadership than in Peter's, but it does happen. Perhaps it happens when God clearly gifts us in certain areas of administration, or intercession, or mercy, but we know that we could do a great job preaching. So we take matters into our own hands, and force our way onto the stage – and the result is awful. Perhaps you didn't even see how awful the result was if your ambition is what drove you to it.

It also happens when a person we know is struggling. We discover that they are being cared for by a number of others, who are as equally equipped to minister to that person as we are, but we decide maybe we could help too. So we push ourselves into that situation and onto that person; they accommodate us, we speak a lot of words trying to help them, and we leave feeling like our ambitious pursuit of them has been beneficial. But we miss the sigh of relief when we are gone.

It happens in that meeting when, on hearing the plans and vision of our leader, we are not convinced they're satisfactory. We know better, we think. We see something that others are clearly missing. So we share why we think the direction is wrong and what we would do. The leader responds strongly and we become upset and bitter. What we miss is the unhealthy motives that caused us to assume we knew better, and which led to us disregarding the time, effort, prayer and hard work that our leader had diligently invested into the work.

AMBITION LURKS IN EVERY LEADER, WAITING TO SABOTAGE OUR PASSION, AND LEAD IT TO A RECKLESS END. PASSION DISSOLVES INTO RECKLESSNESS IF IT IS SPED UP, ENTICED OR MISINFORMED BY AMBITION.

Moving in the right direction

Passion moves toward anonymity and becomes wise, or it moves away from it, toward ambition, and becomes reckless. We all know reckless leaders. They are, for example:

- The boss who fires the employee who didn't do exactly as she instructed.
- The demanding leader who tries to force his way of doing things on everyone else, even though other ways are more efficient.
- The volunteer leader who didn't get things her way and threatened to quit.
- The disciple who draws his sword and cuts off a servant's ear, because things seemed out of his control.

Perhaps you've been that person.

How do we move our passion toward wisdom, ensuring that it doesn't become reckless?

Following Peter's example

When Peter pulled his sword, the words Jesus had said to him a year or so earlier were likely to have been swirling around his head.

At that previous time, the disciples, led by Jesus, found themselves in the region of Caesarea Philippi. Jesus asked the disciples who they thought He was and Peter shot to the top of the class with his answer. Jesus responded, 'Blessed are you, Simon son of Jonah, for this was not revealed to you by flesh and blood, but by my Father in heaven. And I tell you that you are Peter, and on this rock I will build my church, and the gates of Hades will not overcome it.' (Mt 16:17–18) As Peter reflected on that conversation over the weeks, months and year that followed, he would have revelled in it. Jesus had set him aside. Together with his God-given personality, this moment was the anchor point for his passion.

Then, just a year later in the garden, the soldiers descended upon Jesus and Peter felt like the gates of Hades were bearing down on them. It was his task to stop things – after all those nights of pondering what Jesus meant, he now had this opportunity. So Peter acts out of his passion and ambition and the results are reckless.

Fast-forward 30 years and Peter is writing to a group of churches who are intimidated by the presence of Rome, and are experiencing infighting as the new Jewish and Gentile converts jostle for supremacy. Peter writes, 'As you come to him, the living Stone – rejected by humans but chosen by God and precious to him – you also, like living stones, are being built into a spiritual house to be a holy priesthood, offering spiritual sacrifices acceptable to God through Jesus Christ.' (1 Pt 2:4–5)

No doubt, as pen went to papyrus, Peter's thoughts went back to that fateful conversation when Jesus had called him *the rock*. Over 30 years, those words defined Peter, once called Simon. They sustained him through the exciting birth of the early church, and then the onslaught of persecution that followed. Those words that had once impassioned him now matured to give him wisdom, which he offers to these young Christians.

Though you feel the road ahead is tough, Peter acknowledges, God has been building you together. God will sustain you. God is strengthening you, while He dwells among you. Give yourselves entirely to His workmanship, Peter urges them, because he knows the stoneworker can be trusted. Peter lived a life of trusting the One who had shaped his life. He had pursued Him with passion, and the bumps, knocks, shortcomings and failures along the way had all contributed to the wisdom he now led the church with.

At any stage, Peter could have fled from the road of wisdom and taken matters into his own hands. He came so close when, after denying Christ, he returned to his fishing nets and sought to forget everything that had happened. This was reckless you could say, but Christ found him and called him back to wisdom.

The movement of passion towards wisdom

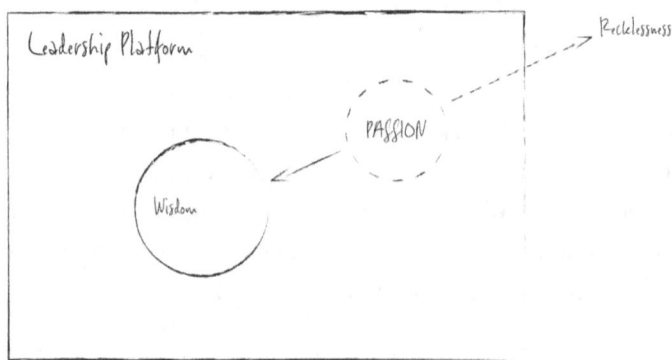

The diagram above shows the movement and direction passion can take. Our passion can migrate toward wisdom or recklessness. Wisdom is at the centre of the platform. Recklessness lies beyond the borders of the God-given platform.

Our passion drifts toward recklessness when we make passionate, uninformed decisions that can invalidate our standing on the platform. Enough smaller reckless acts, or fewer but larger ones, disqualify our leadership as we step clear of the border – which identifies where the platform ends. This movement isn't sudden – any significantly reckless acts have already been telegraphed through many smaller and lesser acts of recklessness.

IF WE STEWARD OUR PASSION TOWARD WISDOM, WE SLOWLY MIGRATE TO THE CENTRE OF THE PLATFORM, AND THE CENTRE OF GOD'S WILL FOR OUR LIVES. BY DOING SO, WE SEE THE PRESENCE OF CHRIST INCREASINGLY FLAVOURING AND DEFINING OUR LEADERSHIP.

The Anonymous Leader seeks to move his passion toward the centre of the platform so he can contribute to the influence Christ might have through him. He realises that if his passion is channelled into wisdom, the decisions he makes result in the Cause of Christ being furthered, and the identity of Christ being seen.

When passion becomes reckless

Youth pastors are renowned for reckless acts that get them into trouble. The same could not be said for me when I was a youth pastor because I was hardly caught – except on one occasion.

It was a Friday afternoon and some of the young women who were a core part of our Student Ministry team had travelled down to the beach, some hours away, to have a girl's retreat for the weekend. Us boys, being boys, thought it would be a great idea to gate-crash the retreat and bring some fun to what was undoubtedly going to be a boring weekend for the girls without us there.

The problem was we didn't have the address of where the girls were staying. As youth pastor, I was volunteered to ask our lead minister for the address. I was also volunteered because the others knew that my passion frequently and comfortably outweighed my wisdom. I knocked on his front door, knowing the girls had left two hours prior, and he invited me in. Not wanting to waste his valuable time, I got straight to the point and asked him for the address.

You spend your life trying to avoid certain sentences – a big one being, 'Hmmm, why don't you come inside for a chat?' My mission wasn't going well.

What followed was a severe reprimand. After establishing why I wanted the address, my lead minister offered, with the utmost clarity, why it would be a foolish and selfish endeavour to visit the girls. He told me what the girls were hoping to achieve during their time away, and what would happen if we interfered. He was very clear on the fencing!

He never said I was reckless, but he may as well have. Then, instead of allowing me to be reckless, he informed my passion with his wisdom.

We didn't go to the beach that afternoon, and the girls had a wonderful weekend away. I absorbed the consequences and saved my friends from the reprimand that awaited them by refusing to give up names. And I came out of the situation with an embarrassed ego and a priceless leadership lesson. Uninformed passion leads to reckless behaviour, and reckless behaviour doesn't just wreck things for me as a leader, but for all of those whom I am seeking to influence.

As an older and slightly wiser leader, I shake my head at how stupid I was. That God dared to stick with me on the platform He gave me, allowing me to influence people, is a miracle of grace in itself. My passion has still not fully migrated to the centre of the platform, but it is on the way. I know I am still in the process of becoming wiser and less reckless, and realise how we choose to steward our passion determines where it moves to.

Stewarding your passion towards wisdom

Here are four thoughts on how you might steward your passion toward wisdom:

- *Get into the orbit of someone who is wiser than you are.* Once you're in their orbit, don't be embarrassed or ashamed at appearing to be stupid in front of them. Don't pretend to be wise for an hour and foolish for the rest of the month. Trust your passion to that person's wisdom.

- *Identify what reckless looks like.* What would be a reckless action for you to take, facing the things you are? What reckless act would disqualify you from your God-given platform? Examine your answer and identify what smaller acts would be contributing factors to the larger act, and then strategise how you will guard yourself against them.

- *Create a regular rhythm of self-reflection.* Wise people reflect a lot. They analyse how they are feeling, what actions they have taken, why they did what they did, and how they reacted to certain pressures, temptations and opportunities. Wise people know how they respond to conflict and what a healthy response looks like. Regularly ask yourself the hard questions, and reflect on your answers.

- *Learn from others.* When people do reckless things, out of embarrassment they will say it was worth it, despite the pain they have been caused. Wisdom will tell you it's not worth it. It's cheaper to buy a book on it, watch a video, or take someone wise out for coffee, than it is to make the same mistake. Leading people is painful enough – you don't need to add to your pain by acting recklessly. Instead, steward your passion toward wisdom by intentionally seeking it out.

10

BUILDING TRUST INTO INTEGRITY

THE VOICE ON the other end of the phone asked me plainly, 'Would you be willing to direct a camp for young people who need respite? Every young person on the list has a sibling or parent with a severe mental or physical disability. The purpose of the camp is to give them a break, with lots of fun. What do you think?'

As the lady spoke, I warmed to the idea. The cause sounded great, a lot of the administration had already been done and the young people were ready to go – they just needed to find a director.

After her sales pitch concluded, I asked when the camp was. After a brief silence on the other end, she replied, 'Umm, well, yes, that's the issue. It's in two weeks' time!' That wasn't much time to assemble a team, organise activities and get a week off the three jobs I had, but it was possible.

It seemed a lot for her to trust me with – I was a stranger, and it had been one phone call – so I asked her, 'Why did you ask me and how did you find me?' It turned out a mutual friend had heard the camp director had resigned and knew a man who might be able to help.

I had been asked to run the camp because a mutual friend trusted that I was trustworthy. Then the woman who phoned me decided she was willing to trust me as well, even though we'd never met and she knew very little about me. The leadership team I gathered around me trusted me. The young people on the camp were going to have to decide whether they could trust me. Again – an essential component of all leadership is trust.

After passion (covered in chapter 9), the second component every leadership initiation features is trust. For someone to lead, someone else dares to trust them.

Increasing the trust in your leadership

There are levels of trust, and every leader either develops or bankrupts theirs. When somebody dares to trust somebody else with the opportunity to lead, they trust the leader will operate with integrity. How the leader then acts affects the future trust in them.

INTEGRITY IS WHAT PEOPLE SEE IN SOMEONE WHO HAS CHARACTER, AND IT IS ESSENTIAL IF THE TRUST OTHERS PLACE IN YOU IS TO BE HONOURED. CHARACTER IS WHAT GUIDES THE TRUST A LEADER HAS ON THE PLATFORM, SO KNOWING YOU CAN TRUST A LEADER IS OF THE UTMOST IMPORTANCE.

If as leaders we judge a person's character based on the recommendation of her friends, we are misled, even if those friends were well meaning. Her friends won't be able to offer a completely accurate appraisal of her character, because the trust that already exists in that relationship will always lean toward a biased evaluation. If we were to ask those friends, inevitably they would say the leader is trustworthy and of good character. If they felt she wasn't, they would likely not be close friends. It's not until a person starts to make influential decisions with those they lead that their character is truly revealed.

Finding leaders we can trust and becoming trustworthy leaders is an essential aspect of leadership. The following tests can help you increase the trust in your leadership, or analyse the trust in another's leadership.

Character test

Character is the most important element to assess in the life of any leader. To do this well, use the following questions to evaluate your past interactions with a leader. You can also direct the questions at yourself to test your own level of trust. Ask:

- Did they do what they said they would?
- Have they lied to you?
- Do they turn up on time?
- Are they reliable?
- Do they fudge the truth or exaggerate?

In asking these questions you're not looking for perfection but self-awareness and realistic understanding. No-one is perfect, and to expect so is to welcome failure. After engaging in these questions, if you find yourself feeling suspicious or uncomfortable about trusting a person, a crack in their character might be why.

Jesus spoke about integrity when the topic of oaths entered into His first sermon. 'All you need to say is simply "Yes" or "No"; anything beyond this comes from the evil one.' (Mt 5:37) He was teaching that our integrity should be of a standard that when we say something it can be fully trusted, because our character can be trusted.

THE LEADER WE ALL SEEK TO BE OR TO FOLLOW IS ONE WE CAN TRUST. THE TRUSTWORTHY LEADER IS THE ANONYMOUS LEADER WHOSE TRUST RATING IS MOVING TOWARD INTEGRITY AND AWAY FROM HYPOCRISY.

This happens as they embrace who they are and the shortcomings they have. If a person is addressing their shortcomings and making progress toward integrity, they are ready to be invited to lead.

Reputation test

If a potential leader passes the character test, it's then important to look at their reputation. What are others saying about this emerging leader? Hypocrisy follows people around like a bad odour. It causes everyone to ask questions, but rarely to the leader's face. If people have concerns about another leader, it's likely you've heard them already. Those concerns are worth listening to. To ignore them is foolish. At this juncture think about what others might be saying about you and your emerging leadership.

I can think of several situations over the years where other leaders whom I trust raised concerns about someone I was about to invite into leadership. They spoke to me respectfully, and about the person in question respectfully. They outlined their concerns and why they held them as concerns, and even named their own bias. They offered their warning well.

Unfortunately, I have not always heeded this wise counsel and, as a result, I have been left burnt and those leaders were disadvantaged. Each time, the cause was an integrity issue. I have grown wiser from these experiences, but am still not infallible. For me, integrity has become an essential quality every leader must have.

In Paul's letter to Timothy, a young leader pastoring a church, he offers a leadership requirement list. At the start of this list, Paul says, 'Now the overseer is to be above reproach'. (1 Tm 3:2) When people look at that person, do they see question marks? Question marks are not good. They represent questions like 'Can that person be trusted?' or 'Will they do what they say they will?' or 'Could I follow someone who treats people like that?' If a leader generates too many large questions marks which hover above their head, it's time to address them.

HOW BIG ARE THE QUESTION MARKS HOVERING OVER A PERSON'S HEAD? WHAT SORT OF QUESTION MARKS MAY BY HOVERING OVER YOUR HEAD? IF A LEADER HAS A SOLID CHARACTER, YOU'LL FIND SMALL ONES, TO ALMOST NONE AT ALL.

Every leader generates some manner of question marks when they lead – it's inevitable. A leader's job is to upset the status quo and when that happens, people get upset. You discover if a leader is above reproach, however, when you start chasing down the questions. If a leader is moving toward integrity, you will find logical, convincing, God-honouring reasons informing their behaviour.

Responsibility test

Every great leader had small beginnings – tasks that were not glorified but necessary to see the Cause advance. How a leader conducts themselves in less significant roles is revealing. How do you react when asked to lead something seemingly insignificant?

Before asking a person to lead something significant, make sure you've asked them to lead something less significant. If this is not possible, interrogate their track record. Ensure they can and are excited to lead something of less significance. If this process causes you to have doubts about their engagement, it is likely a character issue.

THE GREATER THE RESPONSIBILITY A LEADER TAKES ON, THE MORE INTENSE SCRUTINY THEIR CHARACTER WILL HAVE TO ENDURE. IF THEIR INTEGRITY STARTS TO CRUMBLE ON SMALLER TASKS, THIS WILL BE INTENSIFIED AS THE RESPONSIBILITY INCREASES.

These three tests reveal the overall character of a leader. The Anonymous Leader you're looking for, and looking to be, is not mistake-free or perfect. Seeing their weaknesses is far more reassuring than not, and it's important to see how they are under pressure. The question you need to answer is, 'Can they be trusted with more?' Can you be trusted with more? The Anonymous Leader knows it's not about them; it's about the Cause and those they serve. This means they will be eager to do what it takes to be trusted with the Cause.

Trust interacting with failure

Anonymous Leadership is discovered in a leader by how they respond to mistakes and failure. Four indicators identify a potential Anonymous Leader when looking at trust:

1. *An Anonymous Leader will tell you the mistake they've made before you find out.* If is not possible due to circumstances, the Anonymous Leader will still endeavour to approach you about their failure, before you have a chance to approach them.

2. *The Anonymous Leader welcomes correction and seeks it out.* As I write this, an emerging leader I know well comes to mind. Without fail, after leading, preaching, talking or presenting something he eagerly seeks feedback. He's not interested in being told how good he is. He is hungry for critical feedback that will help him do better next time. That's what integrity in leadership looks like. Not a faultless performance, but a hunger to improve for next time.

3. *The Anonymous Leader commits to surrounding themselves with a few trusted, wise people whom they are completely honest with.* They have invited these people into their lives and asked them to bring accountability, impart wisdom and challenge them to grow.

4. *The Anonymous Leader talks about a situation in a way that is the average of what others say about that situation.* Integrity is present when a leader focuses on the truth and not a bias. The Anonymous Leader trusts that the exposure of truth is the best policy.

These four points offer an indication of a person's integrity. They are signposts for us all to move our leadership toward increased integrity, as we move away from hypocrisy.

Understanding integrity

Richard Davis, who has a PhD in management psychology, writes in *The Intangibles of Leadership* that 'Integrity is a multi-dimension construct. It has three main facets: trust, consistency and moral compass.' Integrity always begins with and maintains trust. But this alone is insufficient; you can fool someone into trusting you. Integrity also requires consistency in a person's life. The way you live on the platform of leadership needs to be congruent with both the platform itself and everything you say from the platform. Davis's third facet of integrity is a moral compass.

A moral compass implies direction and movement. Davis tells us that integrity is about choosing what is right, even when the personal cost is high. A leader with integrity chooses to put themselves in a position of self-sacrifice, where they are willing to make sacrifices for the Cause. This is what makes them an Anonymous Leader.

Learning from the example of Moses

Moses is an excellent example of the movement concerning trust toward either integrity or hypocrisy. Moses had found himself as a shepherd in the desert. This position is the equivalent of today's trolley collector in a shopping centre's car park – vital to our shopping experience, but undervalued for what they do.

Moses had been Egyptian royalty until it all slipped through his grasp. Seeing a slave get beaten, Moses intervened and killed the slave driver, was found out and, fearing for his life, fled. Moses wasn't a leader of integrity. He wasn't a leader at all – except for a few dozen sheep he found himself leading around the desert some years later.

Then one day God seizes Moses' attention and future, in the form of a burning bush. God tells Moses that He wants to entrust him with the salvation of His people. Moses isn't sure he should be trusted and argues back, but fails to convince God. As we read the story (found in Exodus) we realise Moses is no longer the young hypocritical man who fled Egypt; he is now a man of integrity.

During that fiery conversation,

> The Lord said, 'I have indeed seen the misery of my people in Egypt. I have heard them crying out because of their slave drivers, and I am concerned about their suffering. So I have come down to rescue them

from the hand of the Egyptians and to bring them up out of that land into a good and spacious land, a land flowing with milk and honey ... And now the cry of the Israelites has reached me, and I have seen the way the Egyptians are oppressing them. So now, go. I am sending you to Pharaoh to bring My people the Israelites out of Egypt.' (Ex 3:7–9)

That is a lot to trust one person with.

God had been watching Moses for the last 40 years. He saw the love of shiny, rich things fade, and the desire for power become redundant. He saw the desert humble a once immature and arrogant young man. He saw Moses' faithfulness in the small things, and his reluctance for glory. God knew Moses could be trusted because his life was moving toward integrity.

For 40 years, Moses had confronted himself on a daily basis as he led his flock around the wilderness. He had become acutely aware of his weaknesses and shortcomings, his flaws and imperfections. He had no motive in this other than discovering who he was and reconciling that with God. Moses had journeyed with God and because of this had grown in his integrity.

Moses is proof that God can shape a person's character toward integrity and away from hypocrisy. The desert forced Moses to come to terms with who he was and accept it.

We constantly see the fruit of this in the story the book of Exodus outlines. Moses faces Pharaoh, the most powerful man in the world, and doesn't flinch. Moses knew who he was and what was at stake. He went to the elders of Israel and, after introducing himself, asked them to trust him. He told them he had heard from God and had come to liberate them. He then walked into the Egyptian royal palace, knowing that could be the end of his life. His thoughts were not about self-preservation or ambition – instead, he was captivated by the importance of the Cause.

Addressing Pharaoh, Moses said, 'The God of the Hebrews has met with us. Now let us take a three-day journey into the wilderness to offer sacrifices to the Lord our God, or he may strike us with plagues or with the sword.' (Ex 5:3) Moses challenges Pharaoh's authority. He has nothing to prove and nothing to hide, and he is not ashamed or worried about anything. He has given himself to the Cause and, come what may, is willing to see it through.

We see Moses' integrity grow as he faces the intense pressure of leadership, indicating it was already strong.

Against all odds, Moses leads the people out of Egypt, through the Red Sea and into the desert he knew. God had liberated His people through Moses and would now lead them through the wilderness.

While in the desert, the Israelites began complaining that they didn't have much to drink. In reaction, Moses took his staff and struck the rock twice to bring forth water for the people of Israel and, in doing so, he violated the specific instructions God had given him. God had told him to speak to the rock, but instead Moses struck it twice. The consequences are grave: '... the Lord said to Moses and Aaron, "Because you did not trust in me enough to honour me as holy in the sight of the Israelites, you will not bring this community into the land I give them."' (Nm 20:4)

Exodus and Numbers are littered with reactions from Moses, the people and God as the three parties strived to live together in harmony. In this instance, however, we don't see any reaction from Moses; he says nothing.

As you read on, you'd be forgiven for thinking it was an over-reaction from God and had been forgotten, as no further mention of it is made – that is, until the time arrives for the people to move into the Promised Land through the river Jordan:

> On that same day the Lord told Moses, 'Go up into the Abarim Range to Mount Nebo in Moab, across from Jericho, and view Canaan, the land I am giving the Israelites as their own possession. There on the mountain that you have climbed you will die and be gathered to your people ... This is because both of you broke faith with me in the presence of the Israelites at the waters of Meribah

Kadesh in the Desert of Zin and because you did not uphold my holiness among the Israelites. Therefore, you will see the land only from a distance; you will not enter the land I am giving to the people of Israel.' (Dt 32:48–52)

There is still no reaction from Moses, no protest at the unfairness that perhaps rages within us when we read it. Instead, he responds by speaking a blessing over the people in chapter 33 of Deuteronomy. He then climbs the mountain, sees the land that he gave his life for and dies.

THE STRENGTH TO RESPOND IN THAT WAY FLOWS OUT OF A LIFE OF INTEGRITY THAT HAS BECOME READY TO SACRIFICE SELF-PRESERVATION FOR THE CAUSE. INTEGRITY OPERATES LIKE THAT. THE LEADER WITH INTEGRITY, AN ANONYMOUS LEADER, HAS TRAINED THEMSELVES TO BE LED BY THEIR CHARACTER BEFORE THEIR HEART.

We see this all through Moses' life as he overcomes all that stood in his way, to fulfil what God had asked him to.

His was a life lived in surrender with no need to prove anything other than what both he and God were already aware of.

The movement of trust towards integrity

Leading on the platform is about living on the platform. It's a long-term arrangement, which is exactly what integrity paves the way for. Just before I began writing this book, a highly respected church pastor of a growing and vibrant church was stepped down. He had disqualified himself from ministry because of too many fractures in his integrity. Then, just before I wrote this chapter, the church world again was rocked by the failings of another high-profile pastor and author. He had engaged in an extramarital affair, citing a breach of integrity, playing out as a reaction to significant marital pressures. Integrity sustains our occupation of the platform but, more than that, for a Christian leader, integrity invites the friendship of God.

Moses had such a strong abiding fellowship with God. He heard from God and sought to honour the directives of God – all because he occupied the platform with integrity. The intimacy Moses enjoyed with God increased as time passed, and Moses' leadership was sustained because of the intimate relationship he and God had cultivated with each other. Integrity leads us into deeper intimacy with God, like nothing else.

INTEGRITY IS AN ABSOLUTE IMPERATIVE FOR GODLY LEADERSHIP. THE ANONYMOUS LEADER CANNOT BECOME ANONYMOUS WITHOUT IT.

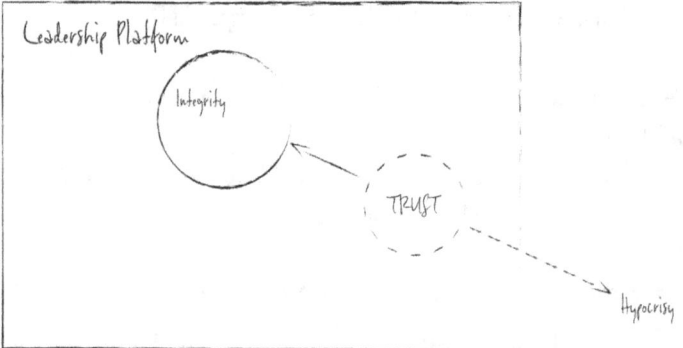

When trust turns hypocritical

When we begin leading on the platform, we do so because someone has trusted us. This trust is not an inexhaustible commodity – it has its borders.

We can abuse trust or fulfil it, but as we fulfil it, it grows into integrity. As trust turns into integrity, we are moved toward the centre of the platform.

Allow me to illustrate by returning to the story that began this chapter. The conversation concluded with my request for 24 hours to decide if I would direct the camp. The next morning I called the woman back and accepted the opportunity to lead a group of young people who didn't know I existed.

The camp was an amazing week that included abseiling, swimming, canoeing, and too many laughs to count. After the camp had concluded, I received a follow-up phone call from the same woman. I told her how the camp went and, thrilled, she asked me to write a report and submit it to the board. A few weeks later I then presented to the board and, after concluding, waited for their feedback. They thanked me, with overwhelming gratitude, for stepping in at the last moment and doing a great job. Then the chairperson said, 'We are so grateful that we could trust you with this initiative. It's made such a difference in the lives of these young people and their families. Thank you for doing everything we hoped you would.'

They recognised integrity in my leadership, which grew out of the trust they had placed in me, and enabled the Cause they had asked us to support to be advanced. They invited us back to run the camp the following year, which I did with the same team, for two more years. Eventually I had to stop, but those camps were some of the most enjoyable camps I've ever directed.

INTEGRITY FURTHERS TRUST, SO THAT EVERY ASPECT OF OUR LEADERSHIP CAN BE TRUSTED. THIS TRUST GROWS BECAUSE IT IS INFUSED WITH INTEGRITY.

Over time I became familiar with the organisation's history and discovered why the previous camp director had been asked to leave (she didn't resign). The board had become tired of parents needing to complain on behalf of their children, mainly because of lack of engagement from the leaders. The leaders hadn't organised activities and didn't care how the young people treated each other. Making matters worse was the poor communication from the director. Questions even emerged about the allotment of camp funds. Frustration levels peaked and in the end the arrangement was concluded.

As I probed into what had taken place, people began to share more information. They reported that the camp director was always convincing them there was nothing to worry about and everything was in order. Nothing could be further from the truth. This leader had stepped off the platform she had been given to direct the camp. She was hiding her true self behind a facade she had created, and working hard to keep others believing in it. She had slipped into hypocrisy.

Hypocrisy is about self-preservation – preservation of your own reputation, status, power, opportunity, money, fame and comfort. Hypocrisy is about preserving a false self in the minds of those who look to and at you, and hypocrisy grows in its prominence when a leader fears losing if the truth is found out.

Hypocrisy is so damaging when it comes to issues of leadership and influence. When someone steps onto the platform they assume a position of trust – their presence on the platform encourages those following to trust them. People then follow, assuming the person they are following is representing the truth. This means the primary responsibility of the leader who invites others into leadership is to ensure integrity is growing.

Once on that platform, a leader benefits from the trust they have been given to influence people. If a leader lacks integrity, they will try to compensate by putting on a mask, desiring to fool those who follow them. As the mask wears thin and evidence to the contrary emerges, a leader finds themselves disqualified from the platform. Their hypocrisy has led them beyond the borders of the opportunity they were trusted with.

The effect of this can be devastating to those who trusted that leader. Their trust in not only the leader but also the Cause that permitted the leader to lead has been shattered. In other words, the leader has tarnished not just their name and reputation but also the Cause they have aligned themselves with.

How many people refuse to come to church because of their perception that Christians are hypocrites? When a Christian lies, not only that person but also Christ loses credibility. When a Christian leader compromises their integrity, the damage is exponential. The damage caused by a breach of integrity is in direct correlation to the extent of influence that leader had.

THE ANONYMOUS LEADER DOES NOT TAKE THIS PATH. SHE STEWARDS THE TRUST SHE HAS RECEIVED AND GROWS IT INTO INTEGRITY. SHE KNOWS THAT AS SHE DOES THIS – AS SHE MOVES TOWARD THE CENTRE OF THE PLATFORM – SHE ALIGNS HER LEADERSHIP WITH JESUS.

Jesus had the most integrity of any person who ever lived. He was God as much as He was man, even calling Himself 'the truth'. Truth is the definition of integrity, meaning that no lie, nothing other than what is true, could be found in Him. This is what the Anonymous Leader moves towards to embrace, and the greater the integrity in a leader's life, the greater the presence of Christ in their influence. We do not need to influence those we lead. The Anonymous Leader seeks for the influence of God to grow in their leadership and define it, and integrity enables this to take place.

Stewarding your trust towards integrity

Here are four thoughts on how you might steward your trust toward integrity:

- *Ensure your actions match your words.* This is the greatest gap in all leadership – well-meaning leaders say one thing and their actions contradict what they just said. Upon acting in this contradictory way, I've heard people say, 'I didn't say that, did I?' They have forgotten what they said or didn't value it at the time. I have learned to value every word I say. I want people to trust my words because they know them to be true. If you find your actions are contradicting your words, go back to the person or people you spoke to and explain why. Doing this enables trust to stay intact.

- *Relinquish the need to be perfect, right or reputable.* Reputable is different from being beyond reproach. Being beyond reproach is to be respected by others because of the way you live. Reputable is to need the respect of others because of the way you live. Let go of the reputation you are seeking or clinging to, and examine your life against Christ. Comparing ourselves against Christ humbles us to see ourselves for who we are. In this position, we are empowered to align our lives to be above reproach.

- *Examine your own behaviour with the intentionality and severity that you apply to others.* The 'fundamental attribution error' is when we excuse our behaviour based on one set of criteria while punishing others for the same behaviour based on a different set of criteria. This only reinforces a gap between our values and behaviour.

- *Gather and remain around people of integrity.* Integrity rubs off on those who are close to it, and it will rub off on you. According to Jim Rohn, you are the average of your five closest friends. If those five people are people of rock-solid character, the trust others have placed in you will effortlessly move to a greater depth of integrity.

11

USHERING INVINCIBILITY INTO HUMILITY

AT 21 I was convinced I was invincible; at 22 I discovered I wasn't. That's what happens when you think you're invincible – one day you find out you're not.

This reality came crashing into my world when I took a group of young people on a bouldering adventure. It was a hot day (32° Celsius or 90° Fahrenheit) and I quickly ran out of water (foolishly I hadn't brought enough). After a few hours I began to realise the consequence of this mistake. I was in trouble. My vision distorted, my tongue began to swell, my head felt light and I grew dizzy.

Somehow we managed to make it back to the bus but all I could find to quench my thirst was an energy drink. I didn't know it at the time, but energy drinks are the worst option to consume if you're dehydrated (because they contain caffeine, a diuretic). Unknowingly, I gulped down the drink and immediately felt worse. We managed to make it home but I was a mess. I drank as much water as I could, fell into bed an hour later and was sick for the rest of the day and night.

In the weeks and months that followed my health changed dramatically. I moved from feeling invincible, bulletproof and indestructible to being frail, weak, dependent and pathetic. The dehydration had weakened my immune system and I caught a stomach virus. The virus created excess stomach acid, which gave me an ulcer, burning through the top of my oesophagus. It took months to reach this diagnosis, as I grew sicker.

The timing could not have been worse. Two months after first becoming sick, I married Lyndal, the girl of my dreams. Our first year of marriage was tough as, although unwell, I continued to study a little and work when I could.

During the full brunt of the sickness, my feelings manifested in clinical depression. No-one likes talking about mental illness – it's more comforting for us to pretend we're all invincible – but doing so helps the healing process.

Depression feels like an inescapable prison that strips you of your self-dignity. You feel more alone than you could imagine, even in spite of the quality and quantity of people surrounding you. It feels like it will go on forever and, as irrational as you are, you feel as though you know what is best for you. It's awful. I don't at all presume to know what the struggle of others is like but I do know what it was like for me. If invincibility was at the one end of the spectrum, my deteriorating mental health had to be at the other.

In the midst of this dark season I went to see a psychologist who specialised in psychotherapy. As we continued to meet, I began to develop clarity about where I was and where I had been. The dominating issue that arose was my sense of invincibility. I had found my value in what I did, not who or whose I was.

AS LONG AS I COULD DO THINGS WELL, I FELT UNSTOPPABLE. PEOPLE LOVED ME, FRIENDS WANTED TO BE NEAR ME AND I FELT GREAT ABOUT MYSELF. I FELT I COULD BE ANYTHING I WANTED TO BE. I WAS INVINCIBLE. UNTIL IT ALL FELL APART.

It took 18 months to climb out of that hell, which only happened by the grace, strength and truth of God. I am thankful for God's grace every day. It is more glorious and wonderful than we will ever fully comprehend.

While that experience was immeasurably painful, what I gained from that season is actually one of my most treasured gifts – the realisation that I am not invincible. I now appreciate my vulnerabilities, and know they help me grow stronger.

Getting to this place took me a while. When I first realised how vulnerable I was, I refused to accept it. I hated it. I wanted to be invincible. I had been told that I could do and be anything I wanted to be and I'd believed it. My downfall was using the wrong measurements and success markers to judge my accomplishments.

What I discovered in the psychologist's office was a gaping weakness I had been feeding for years – a weakness which had grown to the point it began to devour me. I discovered it is much harder and more painful to recover from a weakness when it has injured you rather than when you first identify it.

The nature of invincibility

The journey of the Anonymous Leader is to find your whole identity in Christ. God is the giver of your worth, and He is the only source of affirmation and encouragement you should desire. This is what humility is – realising who you are not, and who God is; realising who you do not have to be, because of who Christ is, and what you do not have to do, because Christ has already done it. Invincibility moves in one of two directions. It moves toward a healthy understanding of ourselves as we are before God (that is, humility) or toward a position where deep down we do not see any need for anyone other than ourselves (pride).

I recently threw out several books that fed the idea of invincibility. They were written to convince their readers that they only need to believe in themselves, and then they can do anything they want.

IF YOU ARE A FOLLOWER OF JESUS YOU DON'T NEED TO BELIEVE IN YOURSELF. GOD BELIEVES IN YOU, AND HE IS FAR GREATER AT IT THAN YOU ARE. ALL YOU NEED TO DO IS BELIEVE IN HIM.

You don't need to worry about yourself, because God is concerned for you – so you're free to enjoy God and journey with God on the adventure He desires to take you on. Why some people limit their belief to just themselves is a tragic mystery – it's tremendously potential-limiting.

The idea of invincibility is born out of self. The word is thought to have derived from a Middle English Latin term, *vincibilis*, meaning 'to be conquered'. The prefix was added to provide the term we have today, invincible: incapable of being overcome or defeated; unconquerable.

Every leader who takes to the platform of leadership thinks they are invincible.

When you first heard that word in this chapter what did you picture? A superhero? Someone who was bulletproof? Unbreakable? The picture in your head is the reason you may have disagreed with my previous statement. But to be invincible is to be without weakness.

EVERY LEADER, WHEN THEY FIRST START TO LEAD, HAS NO INFORMED KNOWLEDGE OF THEIR LEADERSHIP LIMITATIONS BECAUSE THEY HAVE NOT LED BEFORE. ONLY UNDER THE PRESSURE OF LEADERSHIP CAN ONE DISCOVER THEIR LIMITATIONS, OR WEAKNESSES.

Of course, every leader has their weaknesses, but having them and knowing them are two different things.

As an emerging leader grows, he confronts his weaknesses and, in so doing, will make a choice. He can use his weaknesses to enrich and inform his leadership, which produces humility. Or he can avoid, flee from and ignore his weaknesses. This will move him toward pride and, ultimately, destroy his leadership.

When I was 19, my pastor, Ian, asked me what my weaknesses were. I laughed off the question, saying something like, 'As if I've got weaknesses!' To which he said quite sternly, 'If you're going to be an effective leader you need to know your weaknesses.' The world froze for a few minutes as I realised I had no idea what my weaknesses were. If I had been more diligent then in answering this question, I may have avoided the difficult season I mentioned at the start of this chapter.

Examining and interrogating yourself about your own weaknesses is a painstaking task. It's tempting to want to only admit to attractive weaknesses, such as workaholism or over-achieving. Resist the urge because it will not benefit you. The Anonymous Leader knows her weaknesses and, by knowing them, she is empowered.

Know your limits

A wonderful illustration of this component of leadership is in the life of David. David, who would one day be crowned King of the Israelites, God's people, lived a humble life – not only because he was a shepherd, living out in the field with his sheep, but also because of his character.

From a young age, David found himself leading his father's sheep all over the mountains in search of pastures. Those experiences taught him a lot about his weaknesses.

He realised he would be no match for a lion or bear if one came to attack his flock. So he learned how to use a sling, which meant he could stop a bear dead a hundred metres away.

He learned that without God's protection, he risked being attacked on his route – it was God who led him through the valley of the shadow of death, a menacing stretch of ground known to local shepherds.

He learned how to persuade just one sheep to obey the sound of his voice so the rest of the flock would follow. He loved his sheep and knew the value of each one, and he knew that if he ever lost sight of that, both he and his father would be in a great peril.

David was already a self-aware leader, despite never having led a single person. He knew his weaknesses and limitations and how to compensate for them. He realised the weight of responsibility leadership had, so he feared his father and he feared God with a healthy reverence.

One day, David, the youngest of eight, was visiting his three oldest brothers in Sokoh, Judah. They had followed King Saul into war against the Philistines, and David carried with him food supplies to sustain his siblings. After giving them the food, he became transfixed by the strange standoff taking place.

A giant of a man, standing 10 feet tall, yelled insults across the valley at the Israelite army. He was a huge Philistine, dressed in bronze and fully armed. David heard the challenge: a one-on-one battle to the death, winner takes all. As David returned to his flock that evening, he pondered what he had seen and heard. Something within him began to stir.

David knew his limitations and what he was capable of. He knew against that giant of a man he was useless with a spear or sword and would be killed in hand-to-hand combat. As he evaluated the options, it occurred to David that this Philistine giant was similar to the bears he'd faced – bears that were giants in their own right, which he had cut down with his sling before they came too close. He had speed, his sling, and many scalps to his name. Should he dare to take Israel's destiny into his own hands?

Over the next 40 days a stirring in David grew into an unquenchable call to action. Every few days when he visited his brothers he heard this enemy warrior shout blasphemous claims about the God who had been with him since his birth – the God who had protected him on the plains, the God in whom he found his identity. David was swept up into the Cause – not Saul's cause or his brother's cause, but God's Cause. His intent focused into compelling action. Around that 40th day he visited the battle front once more and asked those standing near him, 'Who is this uncircumcised Philistine that he should defy the armies of the living God?' (1 Sm 17:26) David was arrested by the Cause, and he had no choice but to act.

Upon hearing that David was inquiring, Saul summoned him. Before Saul, and aware of his own weaknesses, David said the words that would have silenced all who were present. 'Let no one lose heart on account of this Philistine; your servant will go and fight him ... The Lord who rescued me from the paw of the lion and the paw of the bear will rescue me from the hand of this Philistine.' (1 Sm 17:32, 37)

Had David not seen conflict before, these would have been prideful words. Indeed, his brothers responded harshly to these words, calling him arrogant and prideful. The reality was very different, though – David's whole approach was defined by humility.

When David first led sheep out from the family home, he did so under the careful watch of a mentor – perhaps one of his other brothers. Walking out that first day, he would have felt invincible and indestructible. As the days went by and the challenges grew, the weight of responsibility shifted from his mentor to David. David began to be moulded by the environment. The invincibility he began with was now being honed into humility.

It was this humility that Saul recognised and what caused him to empower David with Israel's fate. He dressed him in the King's own armour, which was a ridiculous sight that revealed more of Saul's insecurity than David's need. David politely declined the armour. He was aware of his abilities, and the armour Saul offered him would only serve as a limitation.

David shows us that knowing our weaknesses empowers us. David knew what he could and couldn't do, which freed him to operate within what he knew his potential to be. He had never fought a man before, but he knew he could triumph. Humility operates as an accurate lens to judge our true ability by.

Pride, on the other hand, inflates a leader, distorting their self-perception. They deceive themselves into thinking they are more capable than they actually are. Their motive is to ensure that their ambition is satisfied and their own agenda is furthered. They know if they can achieve this, their status and reputation will increase in the eyes of others.

Armour free, sling in hand, David ventured onto the battlefield – much to the anger of Goliath. Goliath began hurling insults at David, who positioned himself behind the Cause.

ANONYMOUS LEADERS DO THIS – THEY SHRINK BACK, NOT IN COURAGE, BUT IN OBEDIENCE. THEY

KNOW THAT THE CAUSE THEY ARE FIGHTING FOR IS BIGGER THAN THEY ARE, SO THEY POSITION THEMSELVES BEHIND THE CAUSE. IN THIS WAY, THEIR ACTIONS, WORDS AND DIRECTION ARE RECEIVED AS MORE THAN JUST THEIR CONTRIBUTION.

When a leader stands behind the Cause and moves forward, the Cause is what is seen to advance. Doing this influences the way a leader casts vision, the call to follow they give, and the strategy they champion. It is all about the Cause. If they were to vanish in that moment, the Cause would still advance, and not vanish with that leader. The leader who positions themselves in front of the Cause threatens to damage the Cause through their limitations, instead of enhancing the Cause through the understanding of their weaknesses.

David makes known his Cause before revealing his own identity. 'You come against me with sword and spear and javelin, but I come against you in the name of the Lord Almighty, the God of the armies of Israel, whom you have defied.' (1 Sm 17:45) David is carefree about his own life, laying it down for the Cause: the name and reputation of his God. As this war of words heats up David springs into action. Using his speed and agility, he rushes down the hill to the stream, to pick up some smooth stones.

He loads one into his sling and charges Goliath. To all watching, this act must have looked ridiculous. For David, however, it wasn't a ridiculous act but a humble one. Humility isn't about sitting back and acting passive, quiet or subdued. It isn't settling for talk when action is needed. Humility is about embracing the strengths given to us by God to steward them in a manner that glorifies God.

Upon seeing David move, Goliath raises his sword to crush this small peasant boy. David unleashes his sling and the first stone strikes Goliath in the head. The entire battlefield goes silent before Goliath staggers and falls to the ground.

The Philistines flee and the Israelites, impassioned by this act of selfless heroism, take chase. Their champion had succeeded and beaten the giant, Goliath.

For many, David was the hero but, for David, God was the hero. The Cause he had given his life to, through his humble service, again advanced. The Anonymous Leader doesn't look at what they have done and conclude, 'Look what I have achieved.' No, they celebrate what has been achieved for the Cause. God's reputation, that day in the valley, was re-established. God's name was no longer sullied, and God's reign had increased.

The movement of invincibility towards humility

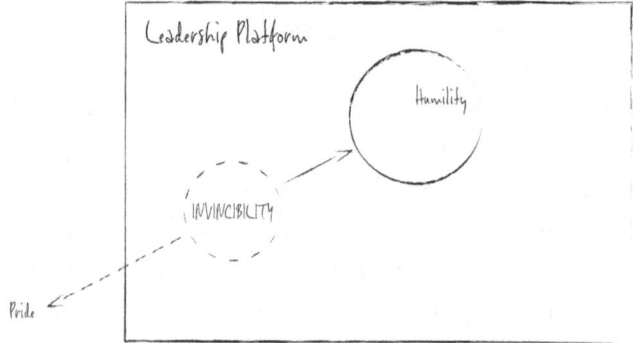

Every leader, when they first start leading, is blind to their weaknesses. This is why all leaders feel invincible when they begin. A leader needs to work hard at identifying their limitations and, in so doing, can be humbled and see God's grace for the valuable gift it is.

In his book *Humilitas*, John Dickson mentions Simon Walker's work in this area. Walker speaks of leaders living in a hostile world and needing to defend themselves. Dickson says, 'Leaders thus imagine that appearing invincible and right is necessary for building loyalty and belief.' Of course, nothing is further from the truth, as both Dickson and Walker agree. Trying to appear invincible to meet a felt threat is an indicator of internal division in that leader. Internal divisions appear when a person attempts to hide their weaknesses and cover up any vulnerabilities. This subverts the humility of a leader and jeopardises the loyalty and belief others might want to invest.

The Anonymous Leader seeks to steward her invincibility to the centre of the platform (see diagram opposite). As humility grows in her leadership, she begins to lead more like Christ. She is able to more easily lay her life down for the sake of the Cause, put aside her ego and think about herself less. Humility enables her to withdraw from public acclaim, because she knows that the advancement of the Cause depends on it.

Some leaders become so caught up in themselves that they steward their invincibility in a different direction. They become convinced they are the person who makes a difference, and dismiss the efforts of others, labelling them as incompetent or unsatisfactory, convinced they can do better. They use God-given opportunities for their own gain, influencing others in an un-Christlike manner. The end result is that people are led by a leader who is aligned not with the Cause but with their own ego and ambition. The ambitious leader violates the permission God gave them when they began leading. When this happens, their pride betrays them.

When invincibility becomes proud

Recognition is something every leader appreciates. It becomes toxic when a leader needs to be recognised. Recognition manifests in a series of questions:

- Did others see me do everything I did?
- Will they tell me how good I am?
- Will they tell me with enough of an audience for it to help me?

- Is this job significant enough for me to do in order that I be recognised for who I am and the contribution I've made?

The need for recognition can taint a leader's influence, causing him to use people and situations to serve his own ambitious needs. Recognition becomes the oxygen that invincibility breathes, causing the heart to become prideful, and potentially disqualifying the leader from his platform.

The need for recognition is a symptom of pride, and it creeps into a leader's soul, often undetected. Its damage, however, is substantial and is the result of undeveloped discipline and surrender in a leader's life. When this type of leader fails to be recognised for work they have done, their feelings can turn to bitterness. Left unchecked, these feelings will change a leader, as he becomes convinced he knows better than everyone else.

Accompanying this is an increasing deafness to God, because God fits in the 'everyone else' category. The outcome is dire. These leaders lead their people in directions different to where God is leading. They become convinced their way is greater than God's, all the while never being able to discern the direction God actually wants to lead them. A leader who fails to address the creep of recognition-need eventually surrenders their influence.

Recognition versus encouragement

Recognition is different to encouragement. A leader desires recognition in order to know their work is worth it. The Anonymous Leader doesn't strive to be recognised. They lead to glorify God who has already recognised them as His child. No further recognition is needed. The difference is in needing recognition for what that person has achieved, versus needing God to be recognised for what He has achieved and offered.

ENCOURAGEMENT IS TO SPEAK COURAGE INTO A PERSON, THAT THEY MIGHT REALISE

WHAT THEY ARE CALLED TO DO. EVERY LEADER NEEDS ENCOURAGEMENT. TO GIVE AND RECEIVE ENCOURAGEMENT COMES FROM HUMILITY, WHILE THE NEED FOR RECOGNITION COMES FROM PRIDE.

In his classic book *Mere Christianity*, CS Lewis said, 'Pride gets no pleasure out of having something, only out of having more of it than the next man ... It is the comparison that makes you proud: the pleasure of being above the rest. Once the element of competition is gone, pride is gone.' Pride develops into an insatiable appetite that drives a leader to strive for ambitious pursuits, leaving him vulnerable to attack.

Pride is when you think you don't need to worry about the things other humble leaders worry about, which is a danger for emerging leaders. Feeling invincible can be a natural state which causes you to not take precautions. Leaders have marital affairs because they never realised they were susceptible and needed to guard against it. Leaders commit financial sin because they never realised they would steal or cheat, so they never guarded against it. Leaders make rash, dangerous and foolish decisions because they always thought they knew best and didn't surround themselves with others who were wiser.

It is easy for a leader to fail to realise their susceptibility to these dangers – sex, money, alcohol, drugs and power all have devastating consequences. Everyone who has ever led is susceptible to these forces – forces which are far greater and far more inexhaustible than any leader is.

Every church can share stories of brilliant, gifted and called individuals who thought they were invincible. They took pride in their invincibility. They refused to create boundaries that might protect them and they strayed well past the borders of the platform, some in spectacular fashion.

Their exit from the platform is often sudden and shocking, yet it is always preceded by a slow migration toward that end. Do not be mistaken. Every leader who has been disqualified migrated there through a thousand smaller decisions. I use the word 'migration' with intention; disqualification is an end toward which an ambitious leader moves at a steady and gradual pace. They increase momentum as they go, until one day the speed is too much, or too public, and the platform is dishonoured.

Invincibility, while serving us to be courageous, take risks and even slay giants, has a dark side. Feeling invincible can lead us to make bad decisions, thinking we are immune to consequence. Our pride blinds us and then destroys us.

In the book of Proverbs we read, 'Pride goes before destruction, a haughty spirit before a fall. Better to be lowly in spirit along with the oppressed than to share plunder with the proud.' (Prv 16:18–19) Pride is what leads us toward, and over, the borders of the platform God has gifted us with. On the other side of that border is a world of pain, which God desperately wants to protect us from. So desperate is God that He has the writer of Proverbs explain the danger to us. He tells us it is more beneficial to be oppressed and not have the opportunity in the first place, than it is to fall. Time and time again, both in Scripture and in human experience, we see leaders painfully fall from the platform. When this occurs, their loss of influence is the least painful aspect. In comparison to this, the damage to their souls, health and families can be irretrievable.

John the Gospel author wrote an epistle to the early church in which he spoke to the subject we are wrestling with. 'Do not love the world or anything in the world. If anyone loves the world, love for the Father is not in them.'(1 Jn 2:15) This wasn't a reference to God's creation but to a Kingdom that stands in opposition to the Kingdom of God. John wants his readers to realise that you cannot stand both in love with God and in love with the world. The gospel writer Matthew would interpret John by saying, you can't stand with one foot in the Kingdom of Heaven and one foot in the Kingdom of the world. By doing so, you are rendering your influence and your life meaningless.

John goes on, 'For everything in the world – the lust of the flesh, the lust of the eyes, and the pride of life – comes not from the Father but from the world. The world and its desires pass away, but whoever does the will of God lives forever.' (1 Jn 2:16–17) Pride distracts our vision. It causes us to lose sight of what God calls us to focus on and start looking for success, meaning, influence, and fulfilment in our own abilities. These can only be serviced in the world, for in God's Kingdom, Christ services our every need.

Pride fuels lust, not just for sex, but for anything which is not yet possessed. This is why John speaks with such stark language. He knows that if lust is present, fulfilment and peace cannot be. If fulfilment and peace are absent, a person does not know the love of God.

What makes us truly invincible

The love of God is what makes a person truly invincible. If she knows that God loves her, and that God is who God has said He is, she has nothing to fear and nothing to want or 'lust' for. If she is free of fear and want, she is unable to be destroyed or broken down. She becomes invincible because of God's love. The irony of this position is that she doesn't need to brag of her invincibility, because it is born of humility. Instead, she is consumed with an unquenchable desire for others to know and receive this gift also. When embraced, God's love causes her focus and vision to shift – from herself and onto others. The result is that she is humbled that God would first love her and then use her.

Stewarding your invincibility towards humility

Here are four thoughts on how you might steward your invincibility toward humility:

- *Find a mentor who will honestly tell you what they see in you, your actions and decisions.* After you find them, give them permission to mentor you. These two steps are essential for your health as a leader. Don't let a leader ask if you'd like to be mentored. Decide who you most want to mentor you, locate them and ask them until they say yes or give you a more appropriate option. Once you've secured a mentor, give them permission to ask you anything they need to. Then commit to absolute honesty. The final step is to commit to contemplating all they say, with the intention to follow through should it prove the best idea.

- *Explore and identify what your strengths and gifts are.* Know them and lean into them. Pride is also thinking that you cannot do something that God has gifted you to do. When a person views themselves in this way, they draw attention away from God and onto themselves. Knowing how good you are, because God made you that way, is as important as knowing what your weaknesses are.

- *Identify the deep-seated appetites present in your heart.* Do you want to be famous? Well liked? Noticed? Appreciated? Comfortable? Free from responsibility? Recognised? The list goes on and on. By identifying the active appetites you have, you can begin to search for the equivalent need that God desires to give you. What are you relying on other than God and His goodness and faithfulness?

- *Develop an intimate knowledge of your weaknesses.* If you don't know what your weaknesses are and what areas you need to guard against, you are inviting disaster. As you develop your leadership, your weaknesses will change, but always know yourself well. Bill Hybels once said that every leader is susceptible to one of the three big temptations: money, sex and power. Know what you are most susceptible to and guard against that with your life.

12

NURTURING CONFIDENCE INTO SECURITY

I HAVE A friend who, for six years, refused to give in to God calling him into ministry. He lived in denial.

If you met him you'd realise God was calling him into ministry too. He loves Jesus, and has a wonderful charisma and a deep compassion. People love to be around him because he understands them. He cares for them and has time for them. If there were a ministry requirement checklist, he would check each box. Yet the thought of ministry terrified him, and he believed the prospect of living out a call to full-time ministry was not for him.

That was until a warm spring evening, when I decided to talk to him again. I called him up and he was happy to hear from me; we chatted about life and all was well. 'So I need to be straight with you,' I soon said. 'I'm calling you for an alternate reason.'

His response was quick, decisive and defiant: 'No.'

'I haven't told you why I called,' I said.

'It doesn't matter,' he replied. 'It's a no.'

'You'd say no so flippantly and quickly to what God might be asking of you?' Silence followed, and then he said, 'Well, when you put it like that, go on, ruin my life.'

So I did.

A ministry opportunity had come up that would fit him perfectly. It matched his skill set, gifts, personality and most definitely his calling. He was the ideal candidate.

In Scripture God insists that we rub shoulders with our brothers and sisters in Christ because we all see more in others than they see in themselves. This is God's way of helping us all realise the potential He has placed in us.

I was confident this emerging leader was the man for the job, except he didn't see it. So in that conversation and in the ones that followed, I spoke confidence into this leader's life. I continued to do so until he was able to recognise the confidence that was within him. It only took six years from that conversation.

IT CAN TAKE A LONG TIME FOR US TO SEE WHAT GOD SEES IN OUR LIFE. HE PUT IT THERE, BUT WE FIND THAT HARD TO BELIEVE, BUT BELIEVE WE MUST. NOT IN OURSELVES, BUT IN WHAT GOD HAS PUT IN US. WE CANNOT LEAD WITHOUT A

CONFIDENCE THAT WE CAN ACHIEVE SOMETHING WORTHWHILE.

As time passed, I saw my friend's confidence become established. He began to believe that he was called. He began to believe instead of fear, which gave him the courage to pursue God's invitation.

When God puts a call on your heart, the last word that can come to mind is confidence – indeed, confidence seems to be a ridiculous exaggeration. Willing maybe, foolish perhaps, but confident seems like the most ill-placed description of what we feel. Instead of feeling confident, we feel daunted.

The reality in fact is this: to take any step toward influencing others requires courage, and courage is born of confidence. When they first begin most leaders don't feel confident. They question themselves, God, their soundness of mind, their decision-making ability. But amid all that doubt, confusion, questioning and chaos, they find the courage to step into the call of God.

Courage is facing and overcoming what was first feared. Confidence enables courage to thrive, and is the belief that a fear can be overcome. One of the components every leader starts leading with is confidence – without it, a person will never find the courage to lead.

Where does your confidence lie?

As a leader matures, what defines their leadership is not their level of confidence, but the source of their security. The Anonymous Leader puts her confidence in Christ. The ambitious leader puts his confidence in himself.

We all sit somewhere on the scale between insecure and secure. Our feelings, of course, are shaped by disappointments and betrayals, broken trust and rejection. But they're also shaped by the amount of love and care we've received, not to mention the sense of belonging and safety we have. With all of these ingredients, it is the heat of ministry that reveals exactly where a leader's confidence lies.

The Apostle Paul exuded a security because his confidence was in Christ. This confidence is captured most profoundly in what became the catchcry of his life: 'For me to live is Christ, but to die is gain.' (Phil 1:21) Paul was undefeatable. His enemies flogged, imprisoned and threatened him, and even attempted to kill him, but it never stopped him. He was bitten by a snake, shipwrecked, engaged in countless conflicts and still he continued on. He was never, as far as we can tell from the Scripture, ever led by his insecurities. His confidence, from the moment he met Jesus on the road to Damascus, was completely fashioned by Christ.

The same Paul wrote to his protégé Timothy, 'Here is a trustworthy saying that deserves full acceptance: Christ Jesus came into the world to save sinners – of whom I am the worst.' (1 Tm 1:15) Paul wasn't intimidated by his sin or shortcomings. He was led deeper into grace because of them.

WITH INCREASING REALISATION OF HIS BROKENNESS AND FALLIBILITY, PAUL PUT MORE AND MORE CONFIDENCE IN CHRIST.

This is why Paul could never be exploited, deterred, or distracted from his call. His weakness drove him to put his confidence in Christ. This meant that he never had to rely on himself, and he never feared the consequences of his own shortcomings and limitations. He wholly trusted in God. He knew his mission was more important to God than it was to him and, without God, would be impossible to fulfil. Paul never spoke about the calling and mission he faced as impossible. He beckons death to approach if it dares.

Luke recalls in the book of Acts a fascinating encounter in Caesarea, with a prophet named Agabus.

> Coming over to us, Agabus took Paul's belt, tied his own hands and feet with it and said, 'The Holy Spirit says, "In this way the Jewish leaders in Jerusalem will bind the owner of this belt and will hand him over to the Gentiles."'
>
> When we heard this, we and the people there pleaded with Paul not to go up to Jerusalem. Then Paul answered, 'Why are you weeping and breaking my heart? I am ready not only to be bound, but also to die in Jerusalem for the name of the Lord Jesus.' When he would not be dissuaded, we gave up and said, 'The Lord's will be done.'
> (Acts 21:10–14)

Paul was never fearful of his insecurities sabotaging him because his confidence was secure in Christ. He knew he was only on the platform of leadership because of God's grace. For him, a self-confessed prisoner of Christ, it was an honour to lead God's mission. (Eph 3:1)

PAUL TEACHES THE ANONYMOUS LEADER THAT WHAT YOU PUT YOUR CONFIDENCE IN WILL DETERMINE THE SECURITY OF YOUR LEADERSHIP.

The search for security in many ways is a long, hard battle, as leadership magnifies your insecurity – you can't be fully aware of what your security is placed in until you feel the pressure of leadership. If a leader is not aware of their insecurities, they can easily discredit themselves. I was awoken to this painfully one day.

When insecurity sabotages you

Within a town I ministered in, some years ago, I belonged to a gathering of pastors. We met together on a semi-regular basis to encourage and pray for one another. One day, I brought to the group some advertising material for a mainline evangelical conference with an impressive line-up of speakers. I was part of the conference leadership team and wanted to encourage others to attend.

After explaining what the conference offered, one of the other pastors started asking questions: 'Why are you going to this?' 'Do you trust these people?' I was taken aback. I answered the questions but left the meeting wondering if I should have offered the invitation at all.

Three days later there was a knock on my door, and I found that pastor from the meeting standing on my doorstep with a large file in his hand. 'Here – take this and read it,' he said. 'I downloaded it from the internet and printed it off for you. You need to read it. Those people speaking at your conference are not who you think they are.' He then walked away, leaving me with a huge pile of uninspiring research to do.

As I began to flick through the pages I realised they were all from antichrist and heretic websites. I was stunned as I read through the pages and looked at the sites. They named everyone from Billy Graham, Mother Teresa, CS Lewis, Henri Nouwen, Karl Barth and John Calvin to more contemporary Christians as heretics.

I was at great odds with the other pastor's Christian worldview.

It became clear to me that, according to the websites, anyone who had done anything for Christ was a heretic – and this included all but one of the nine speakers at the conference I was promoting.

We would need to agree to disagree.

The opportunity to do just that came the following week when he called to see what I thought. I shared with him my response and thanked him for the effort he'd gone to. The conversation concluded as he, slightly disgruntled, farewelled me.

A month later the phone rang, and the caller was a lady I knew well. She was involved in our church and a regular attender. She shared she had just been in a conversation with her friend who attended the same church as the pastor friend of mine. She took a deep breath and recalled the conversation she had just had.

Apparently, in church that morning my pastor friend had warned his congregation about false prophets. In doing so, he identified me as someone who was propagating them, hinting that I might also be in the same camp. This led to a phone call made by a congregation member to the lady in my church to offer her some warning about me.

IT IS ALWAYS BETTER TO RESPOND RATHER THAN TO REACT. WE REACT OUT OF INSECURITY AND RESPOND OUT OF SECURITY. REACTIONS COME FROM EMOTION AND OPPORTUNITY. RESPONSES COME FROM WISDOM AND LOGIC.

I didn't respond; I reacted.

The Apostle Paul would have responded. He was probably featured on that heresy website too, and I don't think it would have bothered him.

Dallas Willard in *Renovation of the Heart* offers four characteristics of a true disciple:

> One is that whenever they are found to be in the wrong they will never defend it – neither to themselves or to others … Another of their characteristics is that they do not feel like they are missing out on something good by not sinning … Following upon these mentioned, is that the children of light are mainly governed by the pull of good … Finally, here, life in the path of rightness becomes easy and joyous.

The reaction you have is a good indicator of the condition of your soul. I discovered in my reaction that my soul was yet to mature into security in Christ. Shameful as it is to admit, I did not at first exhibit what Willard offers as discipleship characteristics.

> **A LEADER WHOSE CONFIDENCE RESTS IN CHRIST FINDS NO NEED TO DEFEND HIMSELF OR HERSELF. INSTEAD THEY RECEIVE ADMONISHMENT AND THANK THE PERSON WHO OFFERED IT. WHEN YOUR CONFIDENCE IS NOT FOUND IN CHRIST, INSECURITY BEGINS TO DIRECT YOUR DECISIONS.**

I didn't realise how insecure I was or how important my reputation was to me. I was more concerned about people knowing the truth about me than the truth about Christ.

My insecurity caused me to react. I wrote an email to my pastor friend. I clearly outlined how I had been wronged and how unacceptable that was. I contemplated sending it to him, to our church members, to his church members, the local paper, to anyone who would read it. Willard said, 'children of light are mainly governed by the pull of good'. Even in my insecurity, good was pulling at me, because Christ was greater than my insecurity. Instead, I deleted the email.

Insecurity is a powerful force in a leader's life. I went from feeling confident in what God had called me to do to feeling like the church I led would collapse around me. All from a ten minute phone call. How can a shift like this happen so quickly? How could I then quickly shift back to a much healthier space after meeting with my church council? My downfall was caused by what I had placed my confidence in. I put confidence in myself, the situation around me, my reputation and my ability to lead – all external factors that are situational. They each change, shift and move as circumstances do.

When you put your confidence in things that are not steadfast, eternal and trustworthy – things that are not secured to anything – your leadership will only ever be as secure as those things are. Misplaced confidence in external insecurities will determine your internal insecurity.

At the time of that incident I had no awareness of my insecurity – like every emerging leader, I needed help in identifying it. If you refuse to increase your awareness of the insecurities you have they will disempower your leadership.

In leadership you need to surround yourself with wiser people than you are. That day, I called a close friend who fitted that description. He helped me navigate through the issue and identify the decisions I needed to make.

I then rang my pastor friend, to respond to what had taken place. I asked him about what I had heard and he confirmed the accuracy of it. We spoke about the ramifications and he offered a half apology, but chose not to withdraw his public remarks. He told me he had not wanted to harm my reputation but to ensure the sanctity of the Word of God. It was a difficult conversation.

The conversation concluded and I was annoyed. Insecure leaders need apologies, because apologies secure the things you place your confidence in. The secure leader does not need or look for apologies; they look for change to take place.

No-one left the church and no-one else mentioned the issue again. People continued to trust me. Insecurity ruins us if we give it fuel – it can ruin relationships, opportunities, our reputation and the teams we're on. It can get us sacked, hated, ignored and avoided. It can increase the amount of conflict in our lives, all for the good of nothing.

The movement of confidence toward security

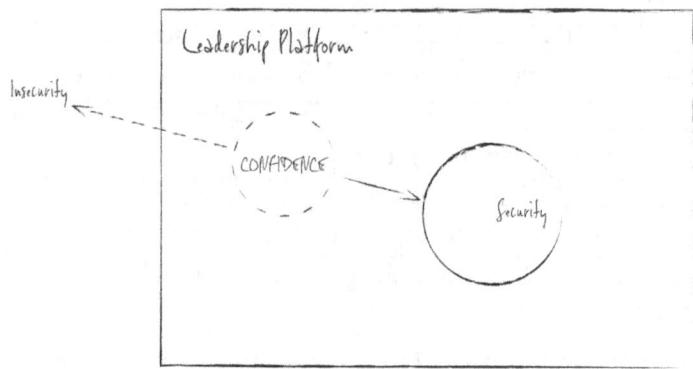

It takes confidence to stand on the platform God gives us, but confidence is integral to leadership. Every Christlike leader who ever occupied the platform put their confidence in God. Confidence is what enabled them to take that first leadership step.

Where your confidence lies is important, even in those first steps of leadership, because who or what you put your confidence in determines the direction your leadership moves in. If you put your confidence in Christ, the reward of communing with Christ is given to you. Communing with Christ is what enables you to follow God's lead, and bring those you lead along with you.

The leader who does this becomes an Anonymous Leader. She moves toward the centre of the platform, establishing her leadership on the will of God. She understands that even though everything else shifts and changes, God does not. God offers the Anonymous Leader a security that cannot be found anywhere else.

Placing your confidence in God

In 446 BC the son of Hacalliah, living in Susa, heard devastating news. The city walls had been destroyed and the gates burnt. A remnant of his people still remained in Jerusalem, the city of his forefathers and the heart of his people, but they were in disgrace.

He says of the news, 'When I heard these things, I sat down and wept. For some days I mourned and fasted and prayed before the God of heaven.' (Neh 1:4) Those days turned into four months.

After four months, the day finally arrived. Nehemiah, the son of Hacalliah, couldn't have known it was *the* day when he awoke that morning to serve as King Artaxerxes' wine taster. As he approached the king with wine – a customary action for a person in Nehemiah's role – the king spoke. 'Why does your face look so sad when you are not ill? This can be nothing but sadness of heart.' (Neh 2:3)

This was the defining moment for Nehemiah. For four months Nehemiah had prayed and fasted, grieving for the city of his people. For four months Nehemiah had grown his confidence praying, 'Lord, the God of heaven, the great and awesome God, who keeps his covenant of love with those who love him and keep his commandments, let your ear be attentive and your eyes open to hear the prayer your servant is praying before you day and night for your servants, the people of Israel.' (Neh 1:5–6) He had been seeking, petitioning, waiting on God. In those four months, Nehemiah's confidence had found its security in God's will. It was God who called Nehemiah, positioned him and gave him a reason to be confident.

Nehemiah was afraid but he spoke up with confidence, telling the king that the city of his forefathers lay in ruin.

And, as Nehemiah stood before King Artaxerxes, he found he was secure on the platform God had created for him.

He was afraid, but he did not let his fear dictate the circumstances. Without fear, there is no need for confidence. Fear caused him to place his confidence in God, and then the security he found in God dictated what happened next.

Nehemiah was an Anonymous Leader, and Anonymous Leaders look at opportunities differently from others. Nehemiah was asked by King

Artaxerxes, 'What is it you want?' Finally he had an opportunity to escape the Persians, maybe even return home. He had spent years in exile; he was a slave himself. He would have dreamt of freedom, but the Cause outweighed it all.

To claim his personal freedom would have been a result of insecurity. If he'd tried, he likely would have been immediately executed.

THAT'S WHAT INSECURITY DOES. IT JEOPARDISES THE CAUSE, AND DECAYS THE ACTUALITY OF OUR GREATEST DESIRES. INSECURITY NEVER DELIVERS ON WHAT WE BECOME FIXATED UPON BECAUSE OF IT.

But Nehemiah was an Anonymous Leader. He existed not for his salvation or freedom, but for God's Cause: the freedom and salvation of others. He confidently answers the king, 'If it pleases the king and if your servant has found favour in his sight, let him send me to the city in Judah where my ancestors are buried so that I can rebuild it.' (Neh 2:5) Nehemiah is granted his freedom and all the resources he needs to rebuild the wall – the wall of the city in the foreign country that the Persians had some years ago sacked.

When confidence becomes insecure

Every leader takes their first step because of confidence, but it is the direction of that step that determines if the leader will have a profound influence for God or a washed-out experience because of their unmanaged insecurities. When you take that step, you either reinforce your security or your insecurity.

SECURITY BELONGS TO THE ANONYMOUS LEADER. SECURITY ENABLES A LEADER TO FADE AWAY – NOT ONLY INTO THE BACKGROUND BUT ALSO OFF THE STAGE. THEIR GREATEST DESIRE IS TO SEE GOD'S AGENDA PROMOTED RATHER THAN THEIR OWN. WHEN YOU PLACE YOUR CONFIDENCE IN THE ONLY IMMOVABLE AND UNCHANGEABLE ENTITY THERE IS, YOU BECOME WILLING TO STEP ASIDE SO THAT ENTITY CAN BE SEEN.

When a leader only finds confidence in themselves, they invest in their fallibilities as well as their strengths. They are putting their hope in weaknesses they know will fail them. As this movement takes place, they move onto their own agenda, doing things that satisfy the needs of their insecurities, and questionable, selfish and blind decisions follow. Their greatest need is not the security of the Cause to which they have been called, but their own security. Instead of heeding God's guidance and aligning themselves with God's desires, they are governed by a need to self-preserve, and this need endangers the Cause.

If this movement continues toward ambition, the leader will forfeit the platform. This can happen in so many ways – from refusing to take risks to move the Cause forward or taking self-preserving shortcuts that compromise important values to becoming manipulative, seeking the fulfilment of personal needs at the cost of those we lead, and refusing to relinquish control and empower others.

Every leader has the capacity to forfeit the platform in these ways. The difference between forfeiting the platform and moving to its centre lies in what we do with our confidence. Are we confident in Christ to redeem our insecurity with his security? Or are we allowing it to put at risk our decisions, our influence and our leadership?

As insecurity takes hold of a leader, their influence changes from serving the greater good to being self-pleasing. This influence violates the expectation of the platform. The two cannot co-exist – the leader needs to change, or they will lose the influence they have enjoyed.

THE ANONYMOUS LEADER CONSTANTLY BATTLES HIS INSECURITIES, SURRENDERING THEM TO CHRIST, IN ORDER TO SERVE THE CAUSE. THIS IS THE TYPE OF LEADERSHIP WORTHY OF THE PLATFORM.

Finding the confidence to pursue the call

The Anonymous Leader's desire is to present Christ to people – this is our primary calling and it needs to define our leadership. We occupy a platform that provides us the opportunity to reveal to others their creator. In order to do this, we need to first be defined by Christ. We need to surrender our insecurities to Him, and know that the worth we have is because of His love for us. Doing this is a risk but one the Anonymous Leader welcomes.

Let's return to my friend at the start of this chapter. It took him six years to find the confidence to step fully into his calling. He volunteered in various churches and ministries but never with an intention to do it for the rest of his life. But with every taste of ministry, his appetite grew and, as his appetite increased, so did his confidence. Until one day the right opportunity arose and, after much wrestling with God, he said 'yes'.

Today he is a leader pastoring people and developing into a very secure leader. He realised that, alone, he was not up to the task of ministry. To pastor anyone, even himself, would not be something he could do without God. Right from his first day of ministry, he put his confidence in God. He would tell you it was God who called him into this life, so the problems in this life are God's to handle through him. He knows any success will only be because of God, and he loves that.

Stewarding your confidence towards security

Here are four thoughts on how you might steward your confidence toward security:

- *Spend time well with God:* To lead well for Christ is to spend time well with Christ. By seeking God each day, we surrender the chance for our insecurities to hijack our influence. We can become nonchalant in doing this when we become familiar with the challenges a role presents. Avoid this at all cost. To keep increasing the security we experience in our leadership, we need to meet with Christ every day.

- *Learn to relinquish control:* We try to control situations because we are scared of what will happen if we're not in control. That is a definition of insecurity. Identify those areas that you need to let go, and let go. In doing so, a freedom will be born in you and in what or who you release. Recognise what you are trying to control and develop strategies to relinquish that control.

- *Ascertain what is important:* Ask, 'What is God telling me is important in this moment?' This question offers clarity, and enables you to move from your agenda to God's. You may struggle to find an answer, so ask someone wise what they think God is saying. It is important as a leader to have others around you who are wiser than you are. Make sure you find them and give them permission to help you identify the insecurities in your life and deal with them.

- *Locate the giver of your worth: Christ* needs to be the giver of your worth. If this is absent in a leader, their insecurities will always compete for attention. Identify where your worth comes from, and reorientate it to Christ. This takes time but it is essential. The worth Christ sees in us is the foundation upon which we become Anonymous Leaders. When my identity is in Christ, I am not shaken by my own insufficiencies. When my identity is found elsewhere, I become defined by these insufficiencies. The danger of this is we can become swallowed up by our own shortcomings.

DRIVING COMMITMENT INTO RESILIENCE

In his book *When the Game is Over, It All Goes Back in the Box*, John Ortberg shares the powerful story of Esther Hillesum. Known as Etty, she was a lovely, brilliant Jewish girl living in Amsterdam in the late 1930s. Her greatest desire was to become an incredible writer, which she had the talent to see happen.

As World War II escalated, Nazi Germany advanced. She had the chance to flee but chose to stay with her people in Amsterdam. She recorded the events that unfolded in her journal, and her writings convey the remarkable transformation of an ambitious woman who longed for freedom, success and recognition into an Anonymous Leader. A person who committed her life to the alleviation of suffering in those she was surrounded by.

She was imprisoned in Auschwitz, one of the more horrific concentration camps. While there, Etty experienced a significant revelation from God, realising that God had created her, and she needed to respond to God so that she might enjoy Him. From that point on, her life became completely enveloped by God as her faith defined who she was. The result was Etty became an invincible and fearless woman.

She was a constant encouragement to those around her, helping them while never fearing what the guards might do to her. Etty moved from entertaining visions of her own grandeur to committing herself to those within the scope of her influence. As this happened, she became resilient against anything the guards tried to impose upon her.

Etty's life was no longer about her. All she now wanted was to bear witness to the goodness and beauty she believed existed even in the hell of Auschwitz. She wrote 'as my soul becomes infinite with God, Nothing can happen to me ... Sometimes when I stand in some corner of the camp, my feet planted on your earth, my eyes raised toward your heaven, tears run down my face, tears of deep emotion and gratitude.'

Gratitude in the face of extreme oppression, anxiety and brutality can only be born of resilience. The more Etty's outer person was enslaved and humiliated, the more her inner self was liberated and made beautiful.

In the final days leading up to Etty's death, she remained deeply concerned about the care and wellbeing of those around her. On her way to her death (in the Auschwitz gas chambers on 30 November 1943), she threw from the train a postcard, etched with her final words.

'We left camp singing.'

Ortberg says, 'The Nazis took control of her possessions, her work, her family, her body, her future, and finally her life, yet she believed that they did not truly take anything at all. Etty responded to God when He called her, she went way beyond mere admiration and her soul soared and was set free – in the midst of hell itself.'

TO WITHSTAND HELL ITSELF REQUIRES MORE THAN JUST COMMITMENT TO A CAUSE. IT NEEDS STEELY, RESOLVED, DEDICATED RESILIENCE – A RESILIENCE THAT REFUSES TO BE MOVED, CHANGED OR SWAYED BY WHATEVER CIRCUMSTANCE CHOOSES TO INFLICT.

Resilience is the deep well that is dug by a continued and unrelenting commitment to the Cause, forged as a person denies the opportunity to quit, and faces the oncoming struggles, dethroning doubt. Resilience declares that quitting is not an option.

Gordon MacDonald said, 'The Christian worships a God who can (and does) take the life of any person, turn it inside out, and use it to build a piece of His Kingdom.' It is during the turning inside out process that a person begins to form resilience. They face who they are and what God is calling them to, and they give their lives to it and put themselves on the line because of it.

Resilience is one of the most treasured prizes a leader can possess. It has the power to sustain through horrendous trials and tribulations, its reward is priceless, and its presence unbreakable. Yet it is birthed through choice.

THE ANONYMOUS LEADER CHOOSES HOW TO STEWARD HIS COMMITMENT. HE CAN CLING TO IT, VALUE IT AND FEED IT, SEEKING TO ALWAYS HONOUR IT. OR HE CAN STARVE IT AND NEGLECT IT, USING IT WHEN IT SUITS HIM AS HE SEEKS TO

SERVICE HIS OWN AMBITION. RESILIENCE IS BORN OUT OF A LIFE LIVED FOR OTHERS.

When life's situations become unbearable, a choice needs to be made. Do I move out from underneath these unbearable circumstances? Sometimes in life this is not possible. When it comes to leadership, however, the option to quit – to fold, run and escape – is always there. The reason we lead determines the choices we make.

Knowing why you lead, and why the things that are important to you are important, is essential to longevity. It is necessary for those who follow you, but it is also necessary for your own sense of purpose. If our *why* is not strong or clear enough, not only will our people opt out over time, but so will we. If we know why it is essential that we remain committed, everything we face is surmountable. The *why* is what helps us dig down deep, and the result of our digging is resilience.

Avoiding the thankless vortex

As I look back on all that God has taught and revealed to me about resilience, I see difficult situations that by God's grace and strength I was guided through and sustained within. The process of gaining resilience always leaves stories and memories such as these in its wake. These stories and memories are a gift, but their price is not cheap.

While I was a youth pastor I experienced a season that felt much harder than others I had journeyed through. Our youth ministry consisted of young people who were committed and loved God; we had a strong core.

One Friday night this all changed, when the core decided to boycott our youth ministry, and stay home, eating pizza and playing video games with their friends. I found out what had happened the following Monday and was both shocked and troubled. I knew these young people, and discipled many of them. It made no sense.

I talked with them and soon discovered the reason for their boycott. They didn't want to come to the youth ministry because they had issues with the way the program operated. They said they were open to talking about these issues so we arranged to meet the following weekend, over food, to navigate a way forward. The group committed to being there.

The meeting time arrived, the food was hot and I was ready. But not one of the 15 young people showed up. This group represented two year levels and 50 per cent of the core young people in our ministry. I was upset.

'I'm done,' I recall saying to Lyndal. 'Those kids just take and take and take. When we give to them, they take some more and throw it back in our face.' I was done.

As that second week after the boycott dragged on, I wondered if we could recover from this. Friday came and these core young people again didn't attend the program. Over the weekend, word leaked out that they had gone to another youth ministry. 'I'm done,' I heard myself saying again.

I had committed so much to these young people, but was it worth all the pain and disappointment? I could be doing plenty of other things with my life, instead of operating in this thankless vortex.

MINISTRY CAN BE A THANKLESS VORTEX IF YOU'RE PERFORMING FOR THE WRONG AUDIENCE. AS I LOOK BACK, I FEAR THAT MY MINISTRY AT THAT TIME WAS A PERFORMANCE TO WOO THOSE YOUNG PEOPLE. I HAD MADE DECISIONS IN ORDER TO APPEASE THEM AND HAD REACTED TO THEIR MANIPULATIVE TACTICS. I'VE SINCE LEARNED THAT MINISTRY IS NEVER TO BE A PERFORMANCE.

Performances are expected when someone stands on a stage to impress their audience. Anonymous Leadership cannot take place on a stage, however – it takes place on a platform and the platform exists to lead people toward a preferred future. A leader who leads from the platform only needs to be concerned with the opinions of one: God.

As the year progressed, some of those young people returned, some left and joined another youth ministry and some fell away from faith altogether. It was tough. What made it worse was how disempowered I felt to effect change. Studies show the average commitment of a youth director is 18 months, because youth ministry is too brutal on the heart (see www.youthministry.com/tag/average-stay-of-a-youth-pastor for more information). I had been in that role for two years at the time, preceded by two five-year terms in two other youth ministries.

Proverbs 4:23 says 'Above all else, guard your heart, for everything you do flows from it.' We guard our hearts by the daily choices we make when faced with adversity. Quitting may feel like it is a method of guarding your heart. It isn't. By quitting you forfeit the very gift God is presenting you with, and which He wants to use to build your resilience. If you choose to cling to your calling, regardless of the obstacles and disappointments, you earn the protection your heart will need as the trials and intensity increase.

At each of those junctures I wanted to quit. I was done, except for one detail.

God had called me to pastor these young people and I knew it in my bones. If I quit, I was not just quitting them, and the young people who remained, but I was also quitting God and, in so doing, quitting the one thing I was put on this earth to do – to walk with those young people through the turbulence of their teenage years and help them to become aware of a God, known as Jesus, who loves them.

I may have – in that season and many times since – wanted to quit, but what I'd committed to was too great to throw away.

THE ANONYMOUS LEADER HOLDS ONTO WHAT GOD HAS CALLED HIM INTO AND TRUSTS THAT IT IS WORTH HIS COMMITMENT. NOT FOR THE EARTHLY RESULTS SEEN, BUT FOR THE UNSEEN HEAVENLY FRUIT THAT IS HARVESTED.

Every leader has an essence of commitment, no matter how shallow. As time passes, obstacles appear that threaten a leader's commitment. Overcoming these obstacles develops resilience, and none more so than in the life of Joseph.

Learning from Joseph

We pick up the story in Genesis 37, when Joseph, a naive 17 year old, goes to talk to his family about a vision he'd just had. It's easy to think of some unkind descriptors to put on Joseph as you read through the beginnings of his adult life. But one thing is for sure, he was a committed young man.

One day Joseph has a dream about his brothers bowing down to him. When he wakes, he seeks them out to tell them about his dream – something that was probably never going to go down well. What made the situation worse was that Joseph was the favourite son, which had been proven by the custom-made, one-off expensive coat his father had made for him. As was to be expected, upon hearing of his dreams his brothers were furious; the division between them and Joseph increased.

As committed as Joseph was, in those early days his commitment wasn't moving toward resilience but toward shallowness. He didn't care about his brothers or the effect his actions would have on them. He didn't care about the ramifications of his decision on his family. He told them about his dream in order to elevate his position in the family – perhaps even to topple the eldest son from his birthright.

One day while his brothers were out working, Joseph was sent to find them by his father. Upon seeing Joseph in the distance, the brothers set in motion a plot to end Joseph once and for all. When Joseph caught up to the brothers, they set upon him, beat him and threw him in a cistern. They were set to kill him until Reuben, one of the brothers, intervened. Just then a caravan of Ishmaelites appeared on the road and the brothers brokered a deal with these slave owners, resulting in Joseph moving from treasured son to shackled slave.

Joseph's journey, chained to a camel and walking behind it, would have been long, hot and revealing as they meandered under the desert sun through to Egypt. We're not told anything of the journey, but it must have given Joseph a lot of time to reflect on his actions and the consequences that emanated from his brothers. Questions like the following must have plagued him: What am I about now? What am I committed to? What is the point of anything? What is going to happen to me? Is this the end – a slow, lonely and painful death in a foreign land?

That journey would have had a significant impact on the shallowness of Joseph's life. After committing himself to advancing through the family ranks, he now found himself committed to a dirt track and the dung that the camel in front of him was producing. He must have felt that it would be easier to give up and die now. Surely he was done! Yet as one foot stepped in front of the other, and as the time slowly passed, he found himself alive in Egypt, where he was sold to the captain of Pharaoh's guard, a man named Potiphar.

A month previously, the last thing Joseph would have imagined he would be was a slave, especially in Egypt. But as Potiphar's slave, he worked hard and was rewarded with respect and honour. He had discovered what he needed to commit to. We're told that 'the Lord was with Joseph and he prospered' (Gn 39:2) in Potiphar's household.

We know Joseph was a man of commitment, and he now invested that commitment not in Potiphar's household, but in God's calling. When the Scripture says that God was with someone, it doesn't only mean that God is with that person, but also that the person is with God. Joseph had discovered anew the God of his fathers and committed himself to God's Cause.

A depth was beginning to grow in Joseph's life. He began to deepen what had previously been shallow, giving his all to the situation he was in. As he set his mind to serving God with all he had, he found that God turned everything he touched into fortune, both for Joseph and Potiphar. As a result, Joseph was put in charge of everything Potiphar owned.

Then disaster struck.

Resilience through God

One day Potiphar's wife beckoned Joseph to join her in bed. He refused, telling her that to do such a wicked thing would be to sin against God. (He doesn't mention Potiphar, just God.)

Joseph's compass had begun to move away from the orientation of people to find a bearing on God, and when a leader's bearing is on God, resilience grows. On this path, sin can be resisted and temptations disempowered – which is exactly what Joseph did. Fleeing the outstretched arms of Potiphar's wife, he headed for the fields.

RESILIENCE, AS IT GROWS, EMPOWERS US TO STAND FIRM IN OUR CONVICTIONS AND NOT SURRENDER TO SHALLOW IMPULSES.

Out in the fields, Joseph was apprehended, arrested and thrown in prison, falsely accused of attempted rape. Here again, God's goodness was present, as Joseph won the kindness of the prison warden. Joseph demonstrates that resilience is the choice to choose God's priorities over our own, and actions like this do nothing but welcome the attention of God, a reward in itself.

The result of such actions highlights for us that the path of resilience is harder in the short term than the other options. The growth that happens within one's self, however, is invaluable.

After more than two years in prison, and interpreting numerous dreams for the King, Joseph was remembered and called for. His mission was to do what no-one else had been able to do: to help the King out with another dream dilemma he was having.

In the previous two years, Joseph had remained committed to God, as he rotted in a prison cell with no hope of release. During that time, God nurtured in him a deep well of resilience that he would later be able to draw on. And we know this because of how he handled Pharaoh's request to interpret the dream.

Thrown before Pharaoh, the situation was explained. 'I cannot do it,' Joseph replied to Pharaoh. 'But God will give Pharaoh the answer he desires.' (Gn 41:16) For Joseph, his dependence on God had only grown. His faith had increased and now, in the face of certain life imprisonment or worse, he leaned on all God had been teaching him. Resilience is what permits a leader to engage with such boldness and steadfastness. Joseph was a man who knew God was trustworthy in any and every situation.

Needless to say, God spoke through Joseph, and the King found peace, having gained insight into his dreams. Joseph was freed from prison and was on his way to becoming prime minister of the entire land, all because of his surrender to the indwelling of God's Spirit.

The problem Joseph then faced was no small challenge. As he had said to Pharaoh:

> God has shown Pharaoh what he is about to do. Seven years of great abundance are coming throughout the land of Egypt, but seven years of famine will follow them. Then all the abundance in Egypt will be forgotten, and the famine will ravage the land. The abundance in the land will not be remembered, because the famine that follows it will be so severe. The reason the dream was given to Pharaoh in two forms

is that the matter has been firmly decided by God, and God will do it soon. (Gn 41:28–32)

To take on such a mission required a leader of resilience, who would not be intimidated by a seven-year famine. A leader who knew what it meant to fight against the elements, and a person who would not be defined or overcome by what raged around him. Joseph was the ideal man for the job. He was committed to God and the well of his resilience now ran deep – it would need to if he was to overcome the greatest challenge he was yet to face.

Resilience paves the way for grace

As the famine hit, neighbouring nations began to starve to death. Hearing of Egypt's great prosperity due to their diligence and forethought, people flooded into Egypt to find food. Among those who flooded in were Joseph's long-lost family.

Joseph's role during the famine was to sell the grain the country had saved, bartering with those who came to buy. Inevitably, he one day found himself face to face with 10 of his 11 brothers, who were asking for food. While Joseph recognised them, they did not recognise him.

The situation must have almost been overwhelming for Joseph. These men, his own flesh and blood, had wanted to kill him but instead had sold him to slave traders. Had he still been the shallow boy he once was, not only would his brothers have been executed on the spot but the nation of Israel would also have been instantly erased. Joseph, however, was no longer a shallow boy but a resilient leader. He was not prepared to let the hurts, disappointments and betrayal of his life determine what the future of God's Cause looked like.

As he interrogated his brothers, Reuben spoke in his native tongue, 'Didn't I tell you not to sin against the boy [meaning Joseph]? But you wouldn't listen! Now we must give an accounting for his blood.' They did not realise that Joseph could understand them, since he was using an interpreter. He turned away from them and began to weep, but then came back and spoke to them again. He had Simeon taken from them and bound before their eyes, and then gave orders to fill their bags with grain, to put each man's silver back in his sack, and to give them provisions for their journey. (Gn 42:22–25)

And so a plan of restoration sprang into motion that was to end with the reuniting of Jacob's family. A plan that Joseph, upon hearing the regret of Reuben and the acknowledgement of their sin, ensured would come to pass.

We've tracked through Joseph's life, witnessing a shallow boy committed to himself and his success mature into an Anonymous Leader.

JOSEPH HAD BECOME A MAN WHO WAS WITH GOD, AND WHO PERSONIFIED RESILIENCE IN THE FACE OF GREAT ADVERSITY. JOSEPH TEACHES US THAT WE TOO CAN DEVELOP RESILIENCE THROUGH THE OBSTACLES WE WILL FACE.

The discipline of preparation

Developing the discipline of preparation gives birth to the resilience required to face the storm. In his excellent work *Great by Choice*, Jim Collins tells the story of two explorers racing to be the first person in modern history to reach the South Pole: Robert Falcon Scott and Roald Amundsen.

These two explorers were the finest of competitors and were matched in every way – except for one difference that set them apart. Spoiler alert: this distinguishing factor enabled Amundsen to be the first man to reach the South Pole while his adversary died trying.

In *Great by Choice*, Collins cites Amundsen's philosophy:

You don't wait until you're in an unexpected storm to discover that you need more strength and endurance. You don't wait until you're shipwrecked to determine if you can eat raw dolphin. You don't wait until you're on the Antarctic journey to become a superb skier and dog-handler. You prepare with intensity, all the time, so that when conditions turn against you, you can draw from a deep reservoir of strength. And equally, you prepare so that when conditions turn in your favour, you can strike hard.

The Anonymous Leader prepares for those harsh seasons where resilience will be needed by disciplining herself – most often out of sight and mind of all others, away from the spotlight and stage. The Anonymous Leader feeds his commitment by establishing a resilient will.

When commitment turns shallow

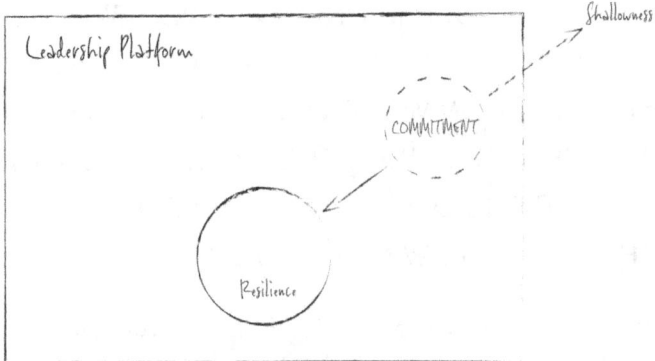

Commitment is one of the five core components in anyone who leads. Everyone who leads is committed to something or someone; however, if that something or someone reinforces a person's ambitious desires, their leadership will drift toward shallowness.

Shallow commitment is defined by a commitment that a person makes to the extent it serves their purposes.

An example of this is when someone is invited to an event, and they accept the invitation and commit to attending. Then, just before the event takes place, the person receives a better offer – an invite to attend a different event. In response to these two offers, the person shifts their commitment from the initial event to the more appealing second offer – sometimes even immediately before the first event commences.

In leadership this tendency manifests in similar ways. Leaders value and commit to people who can benefit them, only to dismiss them when they are of no further use. Shallow commitments are revealed when a person commits to performing a certain task only to withdraw from its execution, citing untrue excuses that mask the true reasons for pulling out.

WHEN A LEADER ACTS TO IMPRESS OTHERS, THEIR COMMITMENT MOVES TOWARD SHALLOWNESS. WHEN A LEADER IS ONLY INVOLVED BECAUSE OF WHAT THEY HOPE TO GET OUT OF IT, THIS SHOWS SHALLOW COMMITMENT. WHEN A LEADER PICKS AND CHOOSES WHAT THEY WILL DO, LEAVING HARDER AND DIRTIER WORK TO OTHERS, THIS IS SHALLOW COMMITMENT.

A clear indicator that a person has a shallow commitment capacity is reflected in the lack of resilience they have. If they are always overwhelmed by stressful situations, are constantly intimidated by small challenges, opt out of things because they seem too demanding and buckle under the pressure of complexity, they lack the resilience of Anonymous Leadership.

If shallow commitment levels drift too far from the initial and expected commitments that have been established, disaster awaits. A shallow leader soon finds themselves stepping outside of the border of the God-given platform they were to steward. More emerging leaders self-select out of leadership via this means than any other method. They gradually disengage to the point they are no longer committed to anything or anyone.

If a person does this with a leadership responsibility, they are also likely to replicate this behaviour in other areas of their lives, including jobs, relationships and other commitments. Leadership is not just about leading people well, but also about doing life with excellence.

What a person in this situation fails to recognise is the damage they do to those whom they are leading. Withdrawing from the commitment they make to leading people is a significant decision, and a commitment shouldn't be forgone simply because of its inconvenience. To do so is to cause those being led and those being served significant damage due to breaches of trust. These breaches can take a lot of time to repair and rebuild, at the expense of those who are given the responsibility to lead in that person's place.

A person is deemed unreliable because they lack the commitment required to fulfil a task. They have chosen to migrate their commitment outside of their influence and, as a result, they forfeit the platform.

This is not the path the Anonymous Leader takes.

Resilience is essential if a leader desires to lead dynamically with long-lasting effect, into the next 10, 20, 30 or more years. And resilience forms as a leader commits herself to the mission God has called her to, pursuing it till God says, 'Enough.'

Jesus is a compelling illustration of this. I am captivated by the story Matthew tells of Jesus' arrest in the garden of Gethsemane under the intimidating shadow of the cross.

After sharing His final meal with His disciples, Jesus goes to the garden to pray. As we explored in chapter 9, His disciples, exhausted, fall asleep only to be woken by Jesus on several occasions. Then the time finally arrives.

> While He was still speaking, Judas, one of the Twelve, arrived. With Him was a large crowd armed with swords and clubs, sent from the chief priests and the elders of the people. Now the betrayer had arranged a signal with them: 'The one I kiss is the man; arrest him.' Going at once to Jesus, Judas said, 'Greetings, Rabbi!' and kissed him. Jesus replied, 'Do what you came for, friend.' (Mt 26:47–50)

The weight on Jesus' heart was staggering. Judas, who He had poured Himself into over the last three years, had now delivered Him into the hands of those who were thirsty for His blood. He knew it was to happen, but still He surrendered Himself to what took place.

Such surrendering requires steely grit – to face such injustice and embrace it. Jesus paints a masterpiece of what resilience looks like. He is taken hold of by the members of the crowd, under the watchful eyes of chief priests and elders. A scuffle breaks out and John tells us that Peter unsheathed his sword and cut off Malchus' ear. At this, Jesus silences the chaos with words that rattled the bones of everyone in the garden.

> Then Jesus said to him, 'Put your sword back in its place, for all who draw the sword will die by the sword. Do you think I cannot call on my Father, and He will at once put at my disposal more than twelve legions of angels? But how then would the Scriptures be fulfilled that say it must happen in this way?' (Mt 26:52–54)

Jesus uses the measurement of 'legion' to convey a very powerful dynamic those surrounding Him would have instantly understood. A few years before this incident took place, Rome had reorganised its military structure and the General of the Roman army now chose how many soldiers made up a legion. Historical records reveal that a legion of Roman soldiers, at that time, could number anywhere up to 16,000 soldiers.

Jesus makes the point that He could access the full and unlimited force of heaven to save Himself. This powerful use of words revealed that Jesus was not going to choose to do what He had every right and power to do.

Instead, He knew the cross was for Him to endure, in order that an even greater victory would be secured.

In His most vulnerable hours, Jesus pressed into His commitment to the mission. He was dedicated to seeing His mission through, embracing the cross and death, so that death would be finished. It is the personification of resilience to welcome death in such a manner. But to submit to what Jesus did reflects the heart of God's commitment to us.

THAT IS WHERE RESILIENCE LEADS US IF WE STEWARD IT WELL: TO THE CENTRE OF THE PLATFORM AND THE CENTRE OF GOD'S HEART.

The key to moving there is to take seriously Clayton Christensen's words: 'Decide what you stand for. And then stand for it all the time.' Shallow leadership provides little influence. People need and deserve to be led by someone who is committed to them, no matter what, through no matter what, and committed to fulfilling the calling God has issued. It is your responsibility to cultivate your commitment and move it toward resilience. As hard as that path will be, you will see it develop resilience in your life, and be so thankful you made that choice.

Moving commitment towards resilience

Here are four thoughts on how you might steward your commitment toward resilience:

- *Clarify your why.* Interrogate what you are doing to discover your *why.* Knowing why you are committed to something has enormous power to keep you committed. The Anonymous Leader doesn't drop commitments because of inconvenience, discomfort or a better offer. Knowing why you made a commitment in the first place helps you resist the temptation to drop it.

- *Surrender yourself to the accountability of others.* This ensures you fulfil what you said you would. It's easy to commit to something but then drop it when a better offer comes along. When you do this you are training yourself to value only what benefits you. This will bring you and others a great deal of pain. When you next commit to doing something, do everything you can to see it through.

- *Don't over-commit yourself.* If you do, you will be shallow in every commitment. You have a finite amount of time and energy to invest in a limited number of initiatives. The more things you invest in, the more sparse your time and energy becomes. If you continue to over-commit yourself, some things will not receive any of your time or energy. Anonymous Leaders under-promise and over-deliver. Make an inventory of all the things you are currently doing and committed to. Then rate your current efforts at fulfilling your commitment to those things – evidenced by you turning up and following through. What needs to be removed from the list to enable you to be more effective? If you do this and follow through, resilience will start to develop in your leadership.

- *Develop the capacity of the well from which you draw.* Experience alone doesn't develop resilience – what you do with that experience does. Are you bringing your commitment before God in prayer? Are you reading the Scriptures, so that God's word might encourage you? Are you debriefing it with trusted mentors, gaining from their wisdom? What are you doing to increase the capacity of your well?

PART III SUMMARY

Every leader who steps onto the platform to lead has five components to what they offer: passion, trust, invincibility, confidence and commitment. How a leader stewards these components determines the strength of influence God is able to have in and through their leadership. The goal of every leader who wants to serve their people with the utmost excellence is to develop wisdom, integrity, humility, security and resilience.

These are the qualities we see defining Christ's life and leadership, and are the qualities we should be constantly aspiring to and developing. Followers long for these qualities in their leaders and the Cause is strengthened and propelled forward when this is so. Take the time you need to answer and work on the suggestions at the close of each chapter in this part, which will help you steward each component of leadership toward an Anonymous quality. For further help and exploration, you can purchase the Anonymous Leader Workbook (which can be found at www.theanonymousleader.com).

As we move into the final part of this book, we're going to look at the trade-offs the Anonymous Leader needs to make and how you can make the right trade at the right time. We will then explore what it means to be called by God to the platform and how we live with such a calling. The final chapter is the most important of the book. It looks at how a leader is daily sustained to lead from the platform, and exactly what they have to do to ensure longevity in their leadership.

PART IV

THE COST

14

THE TRADE-OFF

A GOOD FRIEND, let's call him Max, is a great leader with a humble heart. Max is studying, working more than one job, exploring a call into ministry and is a husband and father of three, so he recently asked me for some insight into getting things done.

We spoke about managing work–life balance to honour God and his family, and issues of time management, increased focus and completing tasks and commitments. It was a hearty conversation with lots of application.

A week later another friend invited me to meet him for coffee. He and Max were meeting and thought to invite me along. I was keen except for one problem: at the start of the week I had allocated that same evening to doing a paper for the master's degree I was completing. I was stuck in a dilemma but I soon decided to do what I learned years ago to do – I made a trade.

IF YOU WANT TO BE A GREAT LEADER, YOU HAVE TO DEVELOP THE DISCIPLINE OF MAKING THE RIGHT TRADE. THE TRADE I'M TALKING ABOUT IS RARELY BETWEEN SOMETHING GOOD AND BAD. UNFORTUNATELY, IT'S OFTEN BETWEEN SOMETHING GOOD AND GREAT.

This means the trade is never easy – it always hurts – but it is the only way you can embrace the things God asks you to. I responded to my friend's offer by explaining I would love to spend time with him, but I had to write a paper for my study. I asked them to let me know when they were doing it again, and apologised for not being able to make it this time. I completed the paper that night, well before the deadline, because I'd allocated time to get it done.

The following week I was again talking to Max. He sheepishly said, 'Remember what we were talking about last week? I think a good strategy I should implement is to study instead of going out with friends.' He was referring to the invitation he accepted that I declined. 'Hmmm maybe,' I said with a wink. We laughed, but it's true. Achieving anything significant requires a substantial trade-off.

I've been making trade-offs for a long time – choosing something great, although often long term, over doing something good and immediate. Some would call this delayed gratification, and it does involve giving yourself and your time to long-term endeavours that you don't immediately see the results of. By repeatedly doing this, you reinforce the platform from which you will lead.

Sometimes the trade-off comes in deciding to learn instead of play. Sometimes it's work instead of friends, or family instead of parties. Sometimes it's self-control instead of popularity, or service instead of position. Sometimes it's excellence over comfort, or reprimand over permission.

Those who don't have a habit of great trading view giving something up as an inconvenience, and they struggle to choose the greater option at the cost of something that's immediately gratifying. They do this because it's hard to see the freedom that trade-offs actually offer. For these people, making a great trade in the moment can feel like a sacrifice, not a benefit – because, of course, choosing discipline now means we immediately miss out on something we could have had.

Finding freedom in the trade-off

I realised the freedom that comes from trade-offs when I started running. For quite some time, running was hard. Getting out of bed early or running late at night, getting off the couch when it was easier to watch TV, pushing myself harder when I wanted to walk – all are trade-offs.

As I continued, however, I discovered a wonderful freedom in running, and in being a runner, and this feeling of freedom and health began to permeate the rest of my life. I made good friends because I ran. I could sleep better at night, and I lost weight and could think more clearly. I felt stronger and faster, and I felt happier more often. Freedom was a gift that running gave me, because of the discipline I invested in it.

The same is true with the trade-offs we make for the sake of the platform we occupy. At the time, this choice feels more like a restriction than a freedom. Yet out of that choice to trade something good for something great, a freedom is gifted to us. We likely don't experience that freedom immediately, but we benefit from it over time as we realise what we are now able to do, because of the trade-offs we've chosen.

Making the right choice

Sometimes we make trade-offs that disservice our leadership development, making them without even realising or meaning to. In doing so, we can creep toward good, or worse, forego great. When we choose good over great, we trade in an opportunity to become who God is calling us to become. We trade in some of the potential the platform has to offer us but, more importantly, others.

Each decision to choose great over good looks different – finishing a paper will not always be a greater option than spending time with friends. It was the right trade-off for me at that time due to a number of other factors. Next time in that situation, however, the greater option could be to go out. The greater option is entirely dependent on all the implications of the decision.

TO KNOW WHICH CHOICE IS THE GREATER OPTION IS TO PUT IT THROUGH THE FILTER OF YOUR CALLING. UNDERSTANDING WHAT GOD IS CALLING YOU TO WILL HELP CLARIFY WHAT DECISION YOU SHOULD MAKE.

Your calling, as we will explore in the next chapter of this book, is your life's *why*, given to you by God. And that *why* represents an infinite number of complex implications for your life – present and future. Each decision you are presented with tests an aspect of your calling. Your task, as you occupy the platform, is to identify the greatest benefit to your calling and pursue that choice. You will know what to choose because it will complement your calling and fulfil what God has been saying to you.

Some questions that will help you make the greater trade when presented with a choice are as follows:

- *Does this choice rebel against what God has called me to?* Opportunities will arise that you know are plain wrong – knowing they are wrong, however, isn't always enough to prevent you from doing them. Putting the choice alongside what you are called to helps you make a great decision.

- *Which choice most aligns me with the heart of Jesus?* Alignment with Christ's heart is a good thing. A similar question might be, what advances the Kingdom of God in my own soul?
- *Which choice fulfils a prior commitment I have already made?* For the Anonymous Leader, a prior commitment trumps a new invitation, except in extreme situations.
- *Which choice has longer term benefits or consequences?* Sometimes the long-term benefits or consequences are hard to judge in the heat of the moment; however, evaluating significant decisions against a ten-year scale is wise. For example, ask yourself, what will my life look like as a result of this decision in ten years' time? (If ten years is too much, use one year.)
- *Do my insecurities need to be silenced, to choose that which I don't want to do?* So often our insecurities fool us into making awful decisions. Are your insecurities sabotaging your decisions?
- *Which choice will help me make greater decisions in the future?* Every trade-off you make now is training you for the next decision you have to make.
- *What is the bigger picture that I may be missing and that, if grasped, would make this decision easier to make?* Sometimes we gain perspective by asking this question.

Trade-offs are necessary if you desire to become a great leader, but these trade-offs need to be consistent, repetitive and wise. Often these choices require trading your present for your future – which is important, because it's more than just your future that is on the line.

EVERY TRADE-OFF YOU MAKE IS NOT FOR YOUR BENEFIT BUT FOR THE BENEFIT OF THOSE YOU LEAD. THE RESPONSIBILITY OF THE ANONYMOUS LEADER IS TO TRADE THEMSELVES FOR THE CAUSE THEY LEAD.

Trading in your potential for greatness

Jesus lived a life of great trade-offs that both inspired and served those God had entrusted to Him. Jesus' mission was to serve God – to give His life so that God and humankind would be reconciled. The day was coming when He would absorb into Himself all sin and, through doing so, disempower sin's pervasive nature once and for all. To achieve this, Jesus had taken off His glorious divinity as He put on a limited humanity and chose to transition from King to servant – the greatest trade-off ever made.

We see an example of how Jesus personified this in one of the final meals He shared with His disciples: 'So Jesus got up from the meal, took off His outer clothing, and wrapped a towel around His waist. After that, He poured water into a basin and began to wash His disciples' feet, drying them with the towel that was wrapped around Him.' (Jn 13:4–5) His followers would have been speechless, and unable to comprehend what they were seeing. Jesus' discipline drove Him to teach them another lesson about Anonymous Leadership, using Himself as the example.

Jesus was making a trade as He took on the role of the household servant, and moved from being the most important person in the room to the least. He was teaching the disciples that true greatness can only be seen when it is offered sacrificially for the Cause. Jesus was not governed by the perception of others, and was never concerned about status or reputation. He lived a life of trade-offs. What made Jesus great was His eagerness to trade in His greatness for God's, so that God would be glorified.

The Anonymous Leader needs to make the same trade-off, trading in their potential for greatness for God's, in order that God will be glorified. A leader choosing to invest themselves into God being glorified and not themselves is a disciplined choice. Jesus embraced this in brilliant fashion, empowering us to do the same.

Jesus washing His disciples' feet was an act unheard of in their culture. The 12 struggled with this and Peter, especially, is quite vocal in his resistance. Jesus, however, wanted to give Peter a firsthand experience that He anticipated would shape Peter's leadership. Jesus invited Peter in that moment to make a trade – trading his pride and understanding of Jesus, for Christ's service and grace. Offering this choice was unexpected but revolutionary.

RADICAL TRADE-OFFS CAUSE COUNTERCULTURAL MOVEMENTS. THE KINGDOM OF GOD IS A COUNTER-CULTURAL MOVEMENT THAT CAME OUT OF THE MOST RADICAL TRADE-OFF.

This story of Jesus washing the disciples' feet is a powerful moment – a moment that clearly defined for Peter what leadership trade-offs looked like and would be expected of him.

Understanding long-term investments

Watching Jesus make great trade-offs is what shaped Peter's leadership. Everything he was to do for Christ – be it preaching at Pentecost, healing the sick, leading the church or going on mission – came out of a trade-off he made because he knew Jesus had traded off more for him.

As the early church grew, Peter constantly traded in any chance of being glorified to see God's glory increase (for more on this, read the book of Acts to see Peter's leadership defined by trading his own glory for God's).

Peter traded off everything in order to fulfil God's will for his life. And by making these important trade-offs, he was rewarded with an amazing platform that has influenced the entire church ever since. He occupied that platform until his death, when he made one final trade-off. Historical legend says Peter requested an upside-down crucifixion because he felt unworthy to die in the same manner as Christ.

Everything that took place in Peter's life as the early church grew personified what it meant for a human life to be held captive by the Spirit of God. From healing the blind beggar at the temple gate called Beautiful or arguing with the teachers of the law who had him imprisoned, to preaching throughout Jerusalem or interpreting a vision to welcome in the Gentiles, Peter acted as we would expect to see Jesus act. His presence even led people to bring out their sick so that when Peter's shadow fell across them they would be healed.

PETER'S LIFE WAS A VESSEL FOR THE SPIRIT OF GOD TO OCCUPY AND INFLUENCE. THIS IS THE DESIRE OF EVERY ANONYMOUS LEADER – TO BE SO CAPTURED BY THE SPIRIT OF GOD THAT GOD IS ABLE TO LEAD OTHERS THROUGH THEM. THIS REQUIRES A LIFETIME OF TRADE-OFFS, OFTEN TRADING THE GOOD FOR THE GREAT.

Peter leads us in what it means to be an Anonymous Leader, and he was able to because he learned from the most significant Anonymous Leader this world has ever seen.

What made Jesus the most convincing portrayal of leadership anonymity was what happened after He left.

The trade-off

The movement Jesus founded with 12 members grew in the first few years to over 3000 people. Within 300 years, historians estimate the movement to have increased to 3 million Christians. By 2010, 2000 years later, over 2.2 billion people (a third of the world's population) claimed Jesus Christ as their Lord and Saviour. The influence of Jesus is so significant and compelling, even after His physical departure, He continues to grow His church.

Jesus made incredible trade-offs, culminating in giving His life for ours, to further God's Cause. This leadership is what the God-given platform requires of us – to embrace anonymity so the Cause-giver, God, can be seen and followed, because of our influence.

The trade-offs required by a leader are some of the most difficult aspects of the path a leader walks. This path is often littered with disappointment as trade-offs are made but rewards are not yet seen, especially in the lives and progress of others. Every leader who has led for a year or more will be able to recall stories – stories of people whom they saw such potential in that they made a trade (or many) to see that person step into their potential. Perhaps this trade-off was then thrown back in their face, dismissed, taken for granted, ignored, or fled from. Make no mistake about it: if you're doing it well, leadership is painful. Within your leadership, trade-offs are risky, but essential.

Inherent in making a trade-off is the strong possibility of being taken for granted, used, misunderstood and ostracised. Yet that is what life on the platform includes – a life of risk and service, and being prepared to lay down everything so that Christ might be seen and trusted by someone we lead.

Didn't Jesus make the greatest and most costly trade-off ever? His trade-off was an incredibly risky one, but one which every day He sees the fruit of. Life on the platform consists of excellent trade-offs, ones made in prayerful faith, and through trusting in God's goodness and no-one else's.

AN ANONYMOUS LEADER IS A LEADER WHO MAKES TRADE-OFFS, TRADING IN THE GOOD FOR THE GREAT, SO THAT GOD'S CAUSE MIGHT BE FURTHERED THROUGH THEIR LIFE. SO WONDERFUL IS THE OPPORTUNITY TO LEAD AND INFLUENCE OTHERS THAT WE SHOULD BE EAGER TO TRADE IMMEDIATE GRATIFICATIONS FOR LONG-TERM INVESTMENTS, KNOWING THAT GOD IS ETERNAL AND WILL SEE ALL THINGS COME TO THEIR FULLNESS IN HIS TIME.

15

HEARING YOUR CALLING

THE CALL OF God is a leader's greatest weapon. It will sustain you in times of trials, rally you in times of defeat and fulfil you in times of triumph. To lead without the call is unthinkable.

The call is what holds you to the Cause during those dark seasons when you think of giving up. The call supersedes everything. If you are called in ministry, you can make it; if you aren't called, don't even try.

I am equipped to do so many things with my life, but because of the call I can't imagine doing anything else. God has called me to lead His church and love His people, and this is what I have given my life to. I can do this because of the call; without the call, I couldn't do any of it.

The call is robust and can face all manner of things, but it begins to deteriorate when our character is inadequate – meaning the state of a leader's character can bankrupt, derail, sabotage, destroy and decay a calling. While receiving the call is essential, the call is either set free or imprisoned by the state of a leader's character.

FOR THE ANONYMOUS LEADER, THE QUALITY OF YOUR CHARACTER DETERMINES THE QUANTITY OF YOUR CALLING. IF YOU COMMIT TO DEVELOPING YOUR CHARACTER, GOD WILL CALL YOU TO GREATER AND GREATER THINGS. IF YOU DO NOT PAY ATTENTION TO YOUR CHARACTER AND YOU DRIFT FROM THE PLATFORM, YOU ALSO DRIFT FROM YOUR CALLING.

Many Christian leaders have stood on large stages of influence, only to fall from those stages because of significant character flaws. The stage, created by a leader for themselves, permits these flaws to exist. The God-given platform does not give permission for character insufficiencies. Instead, God's platform – upon which we live and lead – relies on the call of God to bring substance, shape and direction to our lives.

Surrendering to the call means relinquishing everything. When God calls, He calls every part of you – heart, soul, mind and strength – to give your life to Him and His Cause.

In his book *Facing Leviathan: Leadership, Influence, and Creating in a Cultural Storm*, Mark Sayers comments,

> So when God then asks something of us it can be jarring. People who live in a democracy are not used to being told what to do by a king, someone who has the authority to issue a nonnegotiable decree. Our culture of the West is based upon rejection of the divine right of kings, but God remains on His throne. The idea that God would interrupt our agenda, our will, and seemingly trample upon our rights by asking us to something – anything – is deeply troubling to the contemporary person. It is an intrusion on our autonomy.

We do not like surrendering who we are and what we have – doing so is difficult and we are defiant. Sayers acknowledges this and says, 'The leader must surrender their personal and cultural constructs of fairness, submitting and surrendering to God's justice.'

To be called by God is the greatest honour a human being can receive. It is hard thing to accept! By nature, it is countercultural, pushing back against most of what we have been influenced to believe. Yet it is magnificent that God would dare to call us, and trust us with His Kingdom.

The calling of God is the one thing that is worth your life – all of it, right now and forever.

The convergence of call

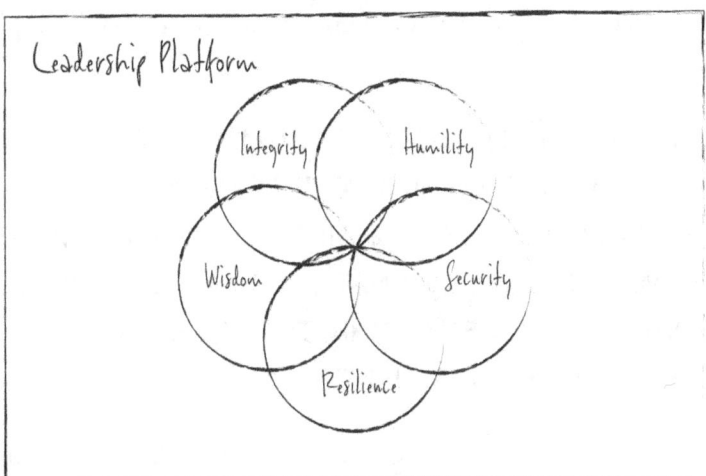

When wisdom, integrity, humility, security and resilience develop (as covered in part III) and converge, the calling in a leader's life gains an unprecedented clarity.

Robert Clinton, in his book *The Making of a Leader*, talks about a leader's life in a series of stages. As the leader grows through these stages, his character is honed, his calling clarified, his gifts sharpened and his experience deepened. The final stage (Phase V) is what Clinton calls the *convergence* stage:

> During Phase V convergence occurs. That is, the leader is moved by God into a role that matches gift-mix, experience, temperament, etc. Geographical location is an important part of convergence. The role not only frees the leader from ministry for which there is no gift, but it also enhances and uses the best that the leader has to offer ... In convergence, being and spiritual authority form the true power base for mature ministry.

The Anonymous Leader reaches maturity when wisdom, integrity, humility, security and resilience converge together. As this happens, the revealed call of God accompanies a spiritual authority that compels people to follow.

A LEADER AT THIS STAGE IS COMPLETELY TRANSPARENT, AND THE ATTRACTIVENESS OF THEIR LEADERSHIP IS CHRIST WHO DWELLS WITHIN THEM. THIS IS A CULMINATION OF A LEADER'S LIFE WORK, AS SHE SEEKS CHRIST FIRST IN EVERY ASPECT OF HER INFLUENCE.

Anonymity is not about being forgotten. It is about realising something far greater as we serve. The service we offer is determined by the call we have. From the first moments, Anonymous Leaders must pursue the call and, as we do, we will find ourselves consumed by it.

My weight of call

On Wednesday 11 December 2002, I was ordained as a Minister in the Uniting Church in Australia. This was the culmination of four years of clarifying the call of God on my life and preparing myself to live it out.

The ordination was an amazing evening, full of celebration, joy, prayer, song and words. What I was not prepared for was the following morning.

I woke up as I normally did but something was different. I felt both physically and spiritually different. Sitting up in bed it was as if a heavy garment had been placed on my shoulders. I felt like the calling was physically resting on my life, and that I had in some strange way been set apart by it. My life had entered a new chapter and would never be the same again.

The calling sets a leader apart to carry a greater responsibility, which is too heavy to bear without God. It is a calling to glory, but not our own. The calling holds a leader to the Cause of glorifying God and extending His reach. It is all encompassing and costs a person everything, but what greater use of a person's life is there?

Elijah was considered to be the greatest of all the prophets, and was charged with the responsibility of finding a replacement for himself. When the time came for him to transfer his mantle of call to another, he wrestled with the enormity of what he was exchanging.

He found Elisha ploughing a field with 12 yoke of oxen and, without so much as an introduction, Elijah walked up to Elisha and threw his cloak around him. This wasn't a strange clothing ritual but a powerful invitation to continue on in the footsteps of the one issuing the invitation. Elisha must have been both elated and terrified, but he left his oxen and ran after Elijah. 'Let me kiss my father and mother goodbye,' he said, 'and then I will come with you.' It was a valid request, given the circumstances and the speed at which things had happened. Elijah agreed, telling Elisha to 'Go back.' We are then given an insight into Elijah's revelation: 'What have I done to you?' (1 Kgs 19:19–20)

'What have I done to you?'

Elijah, more than most, understood the weight and responsibility of the calling of God. He knew what life this would mean for Elisha and, in this moment, we see the magnitude of the call that Elijah was passing on to Elisha.

Elisha left Elijah, went back to his field, took his oxen and slaughtered them. He burned the ploughing equipment to cook the meat, gave it to the people, and they ate. Then he set out to follow Elijah and became his servant. (1 Kgs 19:21)

Elisha responded to a call to leave his life and join God's life. He ensured he had nothing to return to, and gave himself to the call of God. Elisha severed his ties to his family, community and livelihood, abandoning all he knew to embrace the anonymity God was inviting him into. This is the nature of the call of God. It beckons us to leave everything and pursue Christ, with no guarantee of anything.

THE CALL GENERATES A HUNGER THAT CANNOT BE APPEASED – A DEEP LONGING THAT CANNOT BE SATISFIED BY ANYTHING OTHER THAN WHAT CHRIST OFFERS. IT IS A HUNGER TO BE USED BY GOD TO DO HIS WILL. TO BE PLAYED AS AN INSTRUMENT IN GOD'S HANDS, USED AS A TOOL BY A MASTER CRAFTSMAN TO CREATE SOMETHING BEAUTIFUL THAT BENEFITS EVERYONE.

The call, by its very nature, repels us away from selfish ambition towards a selfless life where we might live with no need for recognition, because of what we get to be a part of.

Several chapters later in the second book of Kings, we witness the departure of Elijah. Elisha and Elijah have been moving from city to city, as Elijah prepared to leave Elisha. As a last offering, Elijah says to Elisha, 'Tell me what I can do for you before I am taken from you?' Elisha replies, 'Let me inherit a double portion of your spirit.' (2 Kgs 2:9)

Elisha now knew what God had called him to after he'd journeyed with Elijah. He knew the enormity of the task before him and the calling God had placed on him. This was the moment he began to accept the mantle that had been placed on him earlier.

The call of God works like this – it develops, gradually consuming those who surrender to its pull, growing in its weight as the bearer accepts more and more of its responsibility. The accepting of responsibility unfolds as a leader's character is formed and shaped like Christ. This is what happened for Elisha.

Elijah granted Elisha's request, and then was taken up to heaven in a blazing trail of fire, leaving Elisha to continue on the ministry. After grieving his loss, Elisha picked up Elijah's cloak. This was more than just tidying up after Elijah – Elisha had come to the point of fully accepting the calling of God. The calling is what you grow into, as it grows in you.

Upon accepting the call, Elisha takes the cloak, rolls it up and strikes the water of the River Jordan, through which he and Elijah had just walked in the same manner. The water divided to the right and to the left and Elisha walked through. He was met on the other side by a company of prophets who had witnessed all the recent events. They said to him, 'The spirit of Elijah is resting on Elisha.' Recognising the call of God that now clearly rested on Elisha, they bowed to the ground before him. (2 Kgs 2:13–15)

When a person is called, others can see it. It rests on them just as Elijah's cloak hung from Elisha's shoulders. The call needs to be nurtured, and this nurturing is a process every leader goes through as God forges His calling into the life of that leader; gradually orientating the leader's passion, trust, invincibility, confidence and commitment around it.

The cloak that Elisha accepts from Elijah is not to be confused with the cloak of leadership described in chapter 5. While Elisha accepted a cloak made of material that he would have taken off at times, at the same time he accepted the lifelong call that was symbolised in the cloak; a prophetic platform of influence. Upon Elijah's departure, Elisha stepped toward the centre of the platform that God had given him and Elijah had invited him onto. This was verified by the prophets near Jericho who bowed down to him, paying homage to the call of God that was clearly now resting on Elisha's life.

The morning after my ordination signified my surrender to the call of God. God had been calling me for years leading up to that point, and during that time I had entertained the call and then accepted it, but now had come the point of full surrender to it. Every Anonymous Leader goes through this process of embodying the call of God. It matters not what the calling is to – be it the church, on mission, in the market place or the family. What matters is that each leader surrenders to it.

Handling the challenge of the call

Knowing the invaluable nature of being called has always been a compelling incentive to develop my character, and increase my awareness of God's voice and confidence in what He was asking of me. As I've done this, I've found the strength of my leadership has grown. Just like in Elisha's story, the more permission you give to the call, the stronger you become as a leader.

I am so thankful for the call. I've never demanded or requested to lead anything. Instead, something within me emerges, offering what I can to help people move forward and become all they can be. That is the gift of leadership accompanied by the call of God.

A LEADER STARTS TO LEAD BECAUSE THEY NEED TO APPEASE THE SENSE OF CALLING THAT THEY FEEL DEEP WITHIN THEMSELVES. AS TIME PASSES, THE WEIGHT OF THE CALL INCREASES, AND THIS CHALLENGES THE BEHAVIOUR AND DIRECTION OF PEOPLE'S LIVES.

This challenge can be too much for some. When the sacrifice is too great or the circumstance too uncomfortable, some leaders relinquish the call. This is followed by a time of unsettlement as they experience the call begrudgingly relinquishing them in return. This does not mean that the call is unavailable in the future, but it is also not a given that it will be available. For a time, those who release the call can remain in ministry as the call of God slowly subsides and releases them – this happens to great leaders as well as to the not so great. This invitation from God, and calling to do something great, is squandered; sacrificed all too often on the altar of self-ambition.

The true fullness and reward of the call is reserved for the Anonymous Leader, who is relentless in their pursuit of what God has called them to.

Again – I could do a large number of things with my life, but only one thing is worth giving my life to. This is the calling of God. Without the call, I am doomed in leading; with it, I am defined as a servant who is willing to surrender his glory for the sake of the God he loves. I hope you would dare to join me by surrendering to the call God has for you.

16

EMBRACING 'CHAIR TIME'

IN THE CENTRE of the leadership platform sits a chair, and what happens in that chair determines what influence comes from the platform. The chair symbolises the meeting of the will of God and the will of a leader, and is the point where these two wills are married – fused together in devotion to one another and a greater Cause through spiritual discipline. What happens in that chair determines the condition and impact of the platform. It is not to be underestimated.

Each chair is different. My chair is nothing special – it came from Ikea– but it's comfortable and sits in a prominent position in my study. I sit in this chair each day to meet with God and I call this time my 'chair time' – a phrase I associate with developing spiritual discipline. Some days I have to fight against distraction, business, tiredness or competing interests to get my chair time. But I always ensure I do.

THE PHYSICAL CHAIR IS NOT IMPORTANT. WHAT'S IMPORTANT IS WHAT IT SIGNIFIES. IT IS THE ANCHOR IN MY LIFE, SECURING ME TO GOD'S WILL, AND IT IS THE SOURCE I VISIT THAT ENSURES MY RELATIONSHIP WITH GOD REMAINS VIBRANT. EVERY DAY, MY CHAIR INVITES ME TO MEET WITH GOD, PULLS ME AWAY FROM MY WORK AND OFFERS A SOLACE FROM THE STORMS THAT CAN RAGE AROUND AND WITHIN ME.

When I sit in that chair I have my journal and a pen, my Bible and a hot drink. I enter into the experience as if I were meeting God for a coffee, which is what I am doing.

This daily meeting with God is the heartbeat of my leadership, and the heartbeat of every Anonymous Leader's influence. Without putting aside time to develop and maintain a vibrant relationship with Jesus, how can we expect our leadership to resemble anything close to His?

Embracing 'chair time'

This book came from the chair

The idea for this book came out of my chair time with God. It was 10.34 am on Wednesday, 21 May 2014 when I sat in my chair. I was feeling inundated by the challenges that were before me, so I began to write about them. A short time later I looked at what I had written and felt a sense of defeat. I picked up my Bible to continue reading the story of the early church in Acts. I had committed to reading until something arrested me, and once that happened I would dwell on why it had, asking God to show me how that verse or passage speaks into my situation.

I faced three separate challenges at the time, all with the same theme: a leader was consistently behaving in a manner that was dishonourable before God, and harmful to their influence. The reading that arrested me was Acts 2:14: 'Then Peter stood up with the Eleven, raised his voice and addressed the crowd ...' I wrote the following:

> It was as if this was the commissioning of the 11 remaining disciples. They stood before a public audience – Jews and Gentiles, accusers and sympathisers – and they embraced what it was they believed. It happened this way that the 11 would forever be held to those words, the statements of Scripture that they would use. Even if they might choose to opt out, the public nature of their ministry, their platform, would not allow it. From this day on, the faith they had expressed in a public forum would be what they were known for. For better or worse, this is what they would be known for. It was a forever deal, dependent not on their platform but on their presence – meaning that even if they stepped off their platform they would still always be seen as the ones who stood on that platform. They were forever responsible for the message they proclaimed that day, because they decided to embrace the platform God gave them.

I then did what I do every time I journal. I wrote the word 'WHISPER' in the margin and I waited for what God might say. Sometimes it's a loud impression on my spirit, or a thought completely outside of my consciousness; sometimes it's a meandering conclusion from what I've been thinking. Sometimes nothing happens and that's okay too. After a time of listening and being still, I wrote:

> Take seriously the platform you have. It is a responsibility you have forever, for the glory of God. If the disciples 'failed' they would have tainted the power of God's reputation, polluting the validity of the Kingdom of God. This means that what you do off the platform, or out of the spotlight, is just as important as what you do on the platform as it gives the platform ministry validity and integrity.

I marvelled at the words on my page. Leadership was not something you put on or step into, only to then take off or step out of.

EVERY DAY AFTER THAT FAMOUS PENTECOST SPEECH, PETER WAS UNDERSTOOD AND TREATED AS THOUGH HE WERE ON THE PLATFORM, REPRESENTING GOD.

This breakthrough changed the conversations I was having and the way I looked at leadership. It elevated the calling of God, bringing more understanding to the function and expectations of leadership. It helped me evaluate my own leadership and address areas that were distracting me from the opportunity God had provided.

The value of chair time

So many times I have felt as though God has imparted to me something of priceless value that shapes not only my life but all those God has empowered me to influence through His love.

Because of my chair time, I have something everlasting and eternal to offer as a leader. I don't doubt that I can lead people without God, but I know that I have no chance of enabling them to meet God, fall in love with Him, trust their lives to Him and follow Him, if I am not living in that reality every day. That reality is made accessible to me through my chair time.

THE MORE YOU SIT IN THE CHAIR, THE MORE YOU ARE CHANGED TO BECOME MORE LIKE CHRIST. LIKE FRUIT GROWING ON A TREE, THIS PROCESS IS NOT SOMETHING YOU CAN FORCE OR EVEN MAKE HAPPEN. IT IS THE NATURAL RESULT OF TIME SPENT IN GOD'S PRESENCE.

Dallas Willard is quoted widely as saying, 'One sign of maturity are the thoughts that no longer occur to you.' Spending quality time with God enables the thoughts that are not of Christ to slip away, and be replaced with the mind of Christ.

Chair time has a powerful accumulative effect as you learn to discern the voice of God. The more you become familiar with God's promptings and the more you obey these, the clearer God's impressions become. The more this happens, the more significant and helpful your influence becomes.

You cannot lead at your God-given best without a vibrant relationship with God. You cannot nurture a vibrant relationship with God without praying, reading Scripture, reflecting on what God is saying, corporately worshipping, being around other Godly leaders who are doing the same and without leading someone. It's just not possible.

THE GREATEST CHALLENGE YOU WILL FACE IN ALL YOUR LEADERSHIP IS MAKING TIME TO MEET WITH GOD. IF YOU MEET THIS CHALLENGE, YOU WILL BE ABLE TO MEET ANY OTHER CHALLENGE YOU ENCOUNTER.

If you do not meet this challenge, the other challenges you face will eventually overcome you. It all starts with making the time. Fight for that time to be with God. Don't trouble yourself too much with what it will look like when you get there, just commit to having your chair time every day.

Chair time is so important in keeping hold of who you are. We can only truly know who we are when we dwell in the presence of our creator. In that space He gently reveals to us that which He needs us to know at that time. The more time we spend in that space, the greater our self-knowledge becomes and the more we can effectively lead with anonymity.

If you are able to develop and honour this simple discipline, you will create a channel through which other spiritual disciplines can develop. I have been having chair time for many years now, and this chair time has enabled me to go on a week-long food fast, have a 24-hour silent retreat, set aside a day free of work every week, read the Bible through several times, and enjoy silence and waiting. All of these, if you know me, are violently against my default personality. We are empowered through our chair time to do greater things that nurture the vibrancy of our relationship with Christ.

It is essential that we seek to develop vibrancy in our relationship with God. If our relationship with God is vibrant, we will yearn to be in God's presence. Every Christian leader needs a vibrant relationship with God if they are to honour and remain on the platform. Vibrancy also speaks of life and excitement, movement and joy, and each of these are important aspects of the relationship we have with God. Nurturing a relationship with God is not a passive or unpleasant obligation we meet; rather, it is the best and most exciting investment of not only our time and energy but also our lives.

WHAT MAKES OUR RELATIONSHIP WITH GOD VIBRANT IS HOW GOD REPEATEDLY AFFIRMS HOW MUCH WE MEAN TO HIM. THIS, ABOVE ALL ELSE, IS THE MOST IMPORTANT CORNERSTONE TO EFFECTIVE ANONYMOUS LEADERSHIP.

In *Souvenirs of Solitude: Finding Rest in Abba's Embrace*, Brennan Manning said, 'Lord, when I feel that what I'm doing is insignificant and unimportant, help me to remember that everything I do is significant and important in your eyes, because you love me and you put me here, and no-one else can do what I am doing in exactly the way I do it.' It's in prayer that we realise we are loved. Leading people can distort this truth. When we lead we can begin to think that we are loved because of what we do, or we are not loved because of what we have done. Prayer renews God's love in us. When we seek out chair time and surrender ourselves to it, we should always be reminded of the great love God has for us. If we lead with the assurance that God values us, all that we have to offer is empowered beyond our own ability.

The essentials of chair time

I have found in my leadership that when I have drifted away from spending daily time with God, every other area of my life suffered. Establishing a healthy rhythm of meeting with God needs to be your priority as a leader. There have been plenty of days where I've failed to sit in that chair, sometimes even weeks. I'm not proud of this, but I refuse to feel guilty about it. Guilt would turn this action of faith into an act of work and, in so doing, the beauty and mystery would be lost. If that's you, stop feeling guilty right now. Hang up the guilt and walk away from it; go and sit in your chair to recover.

To help you with your chair time, I have the following suggestions:

- *Start with 15 minutes:* If you aim for too great an amount of time too early, you'll give up too soon. So start small – 15 minutes a day is ideal. The time will fly and you can fit it in anywhere but enough space is created on a daily basis to make a difference. Over time, you can enjoy gradually increasing it.

- *Remove distractions:* Close the door, turn your phone off and notify those you need to that they are not to disturb you. Life moves at a hectic pace and slowing down requires affirmative action. I find it helpful to have a pen and notepad nearby to jot down the things, as they come to mind, that I will need to do when my chair time has come to an end. That way I can move past these things and protect the time I spend with God in my chair.

- *Choose your materials:* I've experimented with an exercise book, smartphone, tablet, computer, leather-bound journal and Moleskine notebook. What tool you choose doesn't matter – just experiment to see what works best for you. Currently I'm taking the advice of a close friend and using a day-to-a-page diary. Find a way to record your insights so that you can look back on them later – in a year's time, for example, you may want to compare what you were doing at the same time a year ago. What you choose might also need to be portable so you can carry it around with you.

- *Know how to read the Bible:* Read the Bible slowly. There is no rush – you don't get extra points in heaven for reading it quickly or even the whole thing. Chew it over as you read it. Enjoy it. Take note of things you haven't noticed before. Let it speak to you. Honour the Scriptures. Don't feel like you have to read the same version every time either – each has its strengths and weaknesses. You may find an audio Bible is more helpful for you if you are an auditory learner. Take the time to memorise verses that grab your attention and speak to you. This practice will be hugely beneficial to you when leading people and having to provide them with wisdom. You won't have to stop and search – the words will be in your heart and mind, ready to share.

- *Choose any chair:* The chair you choose isn't significant. It may be a seat on the train or in your favourite cafe. It might be down at the beach, in a rainforest or up a mountain. It might be part of your daily commute or while you're lying in bed. It might be each of these things on a different day. Chair time is a metaphor to give you space to meet with God.

- *Don't forget to listen:* A vibrant relationship with God is born out of what God speaks to you. It is possible to meet with God every day and never stop yourself to listen for what He wants to say to you. Each day, make sure you leave space to quiet yourself and listen for what God might be saying. The more you wait for Him to speak, the easier it will be to hear His voice.

The Anonymous Leader leads from the chair that occupies the centre of the platform. In the chair the leader enjoys a vibrant relationship with God that constantly revitalises the rest of his life. You owe those you lead the best leadership you can offer, and that is only possible if you lead from the chair. Build time in the chair into your daily schedule and watch as God builds Himself into your influence.

PART IV SUMMARY

Leading people from the platform is a beautiful mix of exhilarating joy and heartbreaking defeat. It requires you to give up everything and, in so doing, you gain everything. God leads you, if you are willing, toward anonymity where you actually find yourself.

It is a remarkable journey of trading off really good things in order to give your life and decisions to the greatest thing – a decision that at the time can feel near impossible but, when you look back, reassures you it was an excellent choice. Making trade-offs for God is a daily opportunity to clarify and celebrate our calling.

The calling is what anchors leaders to the Cause, and gives them the strength to hold on through the tough times. Being called is the key to it all. Every great Christian leader who ever stepped onto the platform did so because God invited them – called them – to participate in something greater than they could ever imagine.

All this, however, is a short-lived reality if we don't fight to spend time in the chair every day. Being sustained by God is what sustains our leadership. Being directed by God is what enables us to give vision to our people. Being aware we are loved by God means we can lead free of other's opinions and conjecture. This is what enables us to be truly anonymous – when the only audience that matters is God!

EPILOGUE

I HOPE THIS book has helped you identify that the influence you have is because God has given it to you and entrusted you with its use. How you steward God's influence will determine the impact your leadership has – this, more so than the ministry you are in or platform you occupy, determines the faithfulness of your leadership.

If you're not yet the leader you want to be, good. None of us should be. Pay attention to the hunger you feel deep inside to be the greatest leader you can be; feed it and it will grow. Don't be disheartened, because we all started in the same place – standing on a platform that God gave us, passionate for His Cause, and willing to give our lives to it.

God doesn't want you to be incredible; He just wants you to be faithful. If you are faithful, He will be incredible through you.

Faithfulness leads us to cherish the opportunities we are in the midst of and not grow tired or frustrated with them. I trust you are refreshed, knowing that what you are doing is what God needs you to do, and that God is using where you are now to transform your character into that of His son, Jesus.

The size of your platform is not important – after all, it's not yours. Trust in the One who provided you with the opportunity and He will use you to help people as He sees fit. Don't be hurt that you don't have greater opportunities yet. God wants to teach you where you're at and then lead you forward.

At times when you discredit the platform you have, because it doesn't have the reach you'd like, remember that God has you on it for a reason, so find the chair that sits in the middle of it and reconnect with Jesus. A vibrant relationship with your Maker is the only thing that will sustain your life on the platform.

The platform needs leaders who are hungry to make a difference, while knowing it is only God who makes the difference through them. The greatest thing you can do as a leader is seek anonymity while serving God and His Cause with all you have.

I have the honour in sharing with people every day as they strive to honour God with their lives. I am a pastor. I love the people whom I lead and every day feel the immense privilege it is to lead and help them. So I offer this work to you, out of the calling God has placed on my life. May it equip you to become the Anonymous Leader God is calling you to become.

Lead the way anonymously, God loves you.
Your friend,
Ralph

FURTHER RESOURCES

THE ANONYMOUS LEADER is epitomised by wisdom, integrity, humility, security and resilience. These five Christlike attributes can only be nurtured and fully developed through intentionality. This means a combination of praying, reading, watching, listening and learning is required in a leader's life on an ongoing basis.

Knowing what to read and what resources to lay your hands on as an emerging leader can be both daunting and frustrating. The list provided here corresponds with the material found in each chapter and offers you some suggested further resources to help you in your development as a leader. The 'challenge level' rating provided doesn't relate to the level of challenge in the book but rather the depth and demand it places on the reader. If you're just starting to lead, begin with the 'easy' options.

CHAPTER 1: Of course you're a leader

The Leadership Mandate by Dan Black
Challenge level: Easy
This eBook is an excellent introduction to what leadership is and how to establish yourself as a leader. Dan has been leading young leaders for a long time and understands leadership and the journey taken by emerging leaders. You should buy this book now.

Courageous Leadership by Bill Hybels
Challenge level: Easy–mid
This is Hybels's most comprehensive writing on leadership, covering a large range of leadership material in a passionate and emotive manner. He campaigns for the importance of leaders leading in the church and cheers them on.

Descending into Greatness by Bill Hybels
Challenge level: Easy–mid
While the book is not primarily about leadership, it is a wonderful call into humility and service. Hybels asks the question, 'Do Christians place God's desires first – or their own?' He then seeks to convince his readers to put Christ first in everything.

Being Leaders: The Nature of Authentic Christian Leadership by Aubrey Malphurs
Challenge level: Mid–hard
Too many churches and parachurch groups operate under secular leadership principles and strategies without considering what Scripture teaches. This book seeks to undo this and present a healthy Christian understanding of leadership.

Influencer: The New Science of Leading Change by Joseph Grenny
Challenge Level: Mid–hard
Whether you're a CEO, a parent, or merely a person who wants to make a difference, you probably wish you had more influence with the people in your life. But most of us think trying to make change happen is too difficult, if not impossible. This book is about moving away from simply coping and towards learning to influence people, and is an excellent resource if this is a key question you're asking.

CHAPTER 2: Defining leadership and anonymity

Soul Cravings by Erwin McManus
Challenge level: Mid
This book is written to a secular audience to prove the existence and love of God without using the Bible. He speaks to issues of intimacy and destiny in a fresh and creative way. If you're after a different read which you can use to talk with people yet to put their faith in Christ, have a look at this.

Growing Leaders by James Lawrence
Challenge level: Hard
This is one of the most comprehensive books I've read on what leadership is, how it works and what it means for Christians seeking to lead. It is thorough and concise, and could easily operate as a textbook for a leadership class.

The Divine Conspiracy by Dallas Willard
Challenge level: Very hard (but worth it, one small bite at a time)
This book is a classic by the late Dallas Willard. In it, he dismisses 'consumer Christianity' and calls people back to the life and beauty of following Jesus.

Realising that this comes at a cost, he makes no apology and reveals the wonder of a life spent following Jesus.

CHAPTER 3: Learning from John the Baptist

The Barbarian Way by Erwin McManus
Challenge level: Easy
Exploring the life of John the Baptist, McManus looks at how we can live with faith but without restraint. It's a captivating, intriguing and short read, with creative insights and emotional appeal.

Integrity by Dr Henry Cloud
Challenge level: Easy–mid
Integrity, more than simple honesty, is the key to success. Cloud talks about how a person with integrity has the ability to pull everything together, and to make it all happen no matter how challenging the circumstances.

The Undefended Leader by Simon Walker
Challenge level: Mid–hard
This one-volume edition of Simon Walker's trilogy of books on 'undefended' leadership addresses leaders in all walks of life. He speaks of a generous leadership springing out of the life you have to offer.

Renovation of the Heart by Dallas Willard
Challenge level: Hard
This book lays out a Biblical foundation for understanding what 'transformation of the spirit' means. Willard invites his readers into a divine process which 'brings every element in our being, working from inside out, into harmony with the will of God'.

CHAPTER 4: Love or insanity?

The Leadership Paradox by Denny Gunderson
Challenge level: Easy–mid
This book refreshingly addresses the tension in Christian leadership between serving and popularity, the two opposing poles every leader is susceptible to. Gunderson seeks to call his readers back to humble service of their King.

My Utmost for His Highest by Oswald Chambers
Challenge level: Mid
Written as a devotional, this powerful little book feeds and nurtures the spirit 365 days of the year. It's a must-have as far as devotional reading goes, and can

be revisited time and time again. I bought this book years ago and still find it quenches the thirsting of my soul by its Godly words.

CHAPTER 5: Cloaks and platforms

Honest to God by Bill Hybels
Challenge level: Easy
This was the first book I read on integrity and was gripped and challenged by it. It helped form in me a foundation of integrity by exploring the extent integrity matters and affects all of our lives. If you are looking for a great book on who you are before God, and how that influences everything you do, this is for you.

The Top Ten Mistakes Leaders Make by Hans Finzel
Challenge level: Easy
The title says it all as Finzel explores ten mistakes ever leader can easily make. It covers the basics well, and doesn't beat you up as a reader. Instead, it is warmly encouraging and challenging.

CHAPTER 6: Fencing in the platform

Leadership Podcasts by Andy Stanley
Challenge level: Easy (20 minutes each episode)
If you listen to one podcast on a regular basis, make it this one. In each 20-minute episode, Stanley is interviewed on various issues of leadership and is absolutely brilliant, helping you to think in ways you'd not yet conceived.

Culture Shift: Transforming Your Church from the Inside Out by Robert Lewis and Wayne Cordeiro
Challenge level: Easy
Speaking from a church leader perspective and wanting to convey the importance of culture, Lewis and Cordeiro offer a great exploration into culture and how a leader can use it to achieve great things.

Visioneering by Andy Stanley
Challenge level: Easy
This book is a comprehensive exploration into developing a vision and seeing it come to its fruition. It begins with the basics and leads you through the potential complexity vision can create. If developing or casting a vision is the crossroads you're at, read this book.

Leading Change by John Kotter
Challenge level: Mid–hard
Published by Harvard Business School, this book is the industry standard on how to do change management well. If you are looking to change things in your ministry, organisation or workplace, consult this book first. Its structure is simple and it's very insightful.

Start with Why by Simon Sinek
Challenge level: Mid–hard
Every leader should read this book before they die. Sinek is a secular writer but brilliantly explores the power of knowing why we do what we do, and how this impacts our leadership. He also has a brilliant and brief talk on www.TED.com called 'How Great Leaders Inspire Action', which is a wonderful introduction to the book.

CHAPTER 7: Fencing in the platform for leaders and teams

Developing the Leader Within You by John C. Maxwell
Challenge level: Easy
After reading *The Anonymous Leader* and Black's book, *The Leadership Mandate*, make sure you purchase Maxwell's book. It covers all the basic skills you need as a leader to start making a difference, and is well reinforced with stories and quotes which will make you think.

Developing the Leaders Around You by John C. Maxwell
Challenge level: Easy
This book will help you lead other leaders. If that is what you are about to do, or are struggling to do, read it! You'll be equipped with where to start, how to navigate this difficult journey and how to excel at what you've been called to do.

Good to Great by Jim Collins
Challenge level: Mid–hard
Jim Collins is the premiere business writer since Peter Drucker. His work is brilliant and helpful to any leader, and this book is a must for any leader wanting to familiarise themselves with a broader range of leadership thought. The book introduces you to many widely-used management and leadership strategies and tools, with solid research to back it up.

CHAPTER 8: Understanding the work of the Holy Spirit

Spiritual Leadership by Henry and Richard Blackaby
Challenge level: Mid

This book powerfully brings together spirituality and leadership. It is a wonderful book and one I would recommend every leader to read. The Blackaby brothers put Christ in the centre of leadership.

Forgotten God by Francis Chan
Challenge level: Mid

Skilfully explaining the Holy Spirit in understandable language, Chan manages to convince his readers of the importance behind the Spirit's place in our lives and ministry. All this is reinforced by real stories from real people living every day in intimate relationship with the Holy Spirit.

Jesus, Continued by JD Greear
Challenge level: Mid–hard

This book openly and honestly wrestles with the third person of the trinity. It combines grounded, orthodox theological understanding with challenging experiential advice as Greer explains how to have a relationship with the Holy Spirit, in a way which will lead to deeper intimacy with God and greater effectiveness in mission.

CHAPTER 9: Migrating passion into wisdom

Axiom by Bill Hybels
Challenge level: Easy

Hybels brings together his best leadership lessons from 30-plus years of leading, distilled into one-line lessons. It's a refreshing and insightful read that gives keen insight into how to lead with excellence.

Next Generation Leader by Andy Stanley
Challenge level: Easy

Stanley writes this to set young leaders on a successful course of leadership. If you're a young adult looking to lead well have a look at this. Covering five essential principles, the book will help you to create a strong foundation to begin leading from.

The Intangibles of Leadership by Richard A Davis
Challenge level: Mid–hard

I loved this book and in recent years have been powerfully impacted by it. It's a compelling look at what separates excellent leaders from the rest. The book examines in very practical detail ten elements of leadership – so, if you've been leading for a while and want to be really stretched, this is the book for you.

CHAPTER 10: Building trust into integrity

***The Heart of a Leader: Insights on the Art of Influence* by Ken Blanchard**
Challenge level: Easy–mid
Blanchard reveals the greatest life and leadership lessons he's learned in his rich career as an educator and business leader. He allows you a front-row seat into learning the things he learnt without the time and energy he had to expend gaining them.

***A Life of Integrity* by Howard Hendricks**
Challenge level: Mid
Hendricks draws on some of the greatest Christian leaders of this day to explore integrity – a vital aspect of leadership. For a wide and deep look into integrity, from a plethora of very qualified authors and leaders, this book is for you.

CHAPTER 11: Ushering invincibility into humility

***Be the Leader You Were Meant to Be: Lessons on Leadership from the Bible* by LeRoy Eims**
Challenge level: Easy
This book examines who you are as a leader and how to cultivate the traits of an effective leader. It is a call to excellence in leadership and a great book to read if you are just starting out as a leader.

***Humilitas* by John Dickson**
Challenge level: Mid
Dickson tracks the impact of Jesus' humility on the world's history and reveals the profound impact Jesus had. He looks at how influential the impact of Jesus' life has been on nearly all aspects of our society that we value today.

***Mere Christianity* by CS Lewis**
Challenge level: Hard (but wonderful)
Written by the author of the Narnia series, this is CS Lewis's masterpiece. Whether you're a Christian or not, this book will enrich your life and blow your mind. It's an absolute classic and a must-read for a timelessly fresh exploration into Christianity.

CHAPTER 12: Nurturing confidence into security

***The 21 Irrefutable Laws of Leadership* by John C. Maxwell**
Challenge level: Easy
This was the book that established John Maxwell as a leadership guru. In this book, he looks at the 21 laws essential to leadership and explores them in an easy and accessible way. It too belongs on the bookshelf of every leader.

Ordering Your Private World **by Gordon MacDonald**
Challenge level: Mid
MacDonald is a master of self-leadership and has authored many books on the subject. This book is one of his earliest and finest. Reading it, you will be challenged and equipped to re-order your life in a healthy and life-giving way.

Soul Keeping **by John Ortberg**
Challenge level: Mid
This is both a tribute to Dallas Willard and a peaceful delving into what it means to keep your soul whole. Ortberg shares from his friendship with Willard and the profound impact Willard had on him. It is a wonderful read and great for replenishing your soul – read it slowly and deeply.

CHAPTER 13: Driving commitment into resilience

A Resilient Life **by Gordon MacDonald**
Challenge level: Mid
MacDonald writes from his vast experience of church pastoring to share how he developed resilience over the years. His writes from his own life and experience and offers some grandfatherly conviction that will stir your soul toward developing resilience.

Great by Choice **by Jim Collins and Morten T. Hansen**
Challenge level: Mid–hard
Collins, author of *Good to Great* and *Built to Last,* isn't a Christian but his research and work very effectively applies to the social sector. This book, as he teams up with Hansen, will help you refine what you need to do to make great decisions about your leadership and life.

CHAPTER 14: The trade-off

Getting Things Done **by David Allen**
Challenge level: Tedious but necessary
This book provides its readers with a system to get everything done. It's unlikely you'll adopt every system he talks about into your life, but you will be benefitted ten times the price of the book if you read it and implement some of his strategies. It will absolutely help you get things done and become far more dependable and reliable.

Leading on Empty by Wayne Cordeiro
Challenge level: Easy–mid
Speaking from his burnout experience, Cordeiro offers some very pastoral and wise insight to help every leader avoid the same fate. He outlines what happened to him, why it happened and what he should have done about it, as he seeks to encourage you to learn from his failings.

Margin by Richard Swenson
Challenge level: Mid
Swenson is a medical doctor who writes to equip his readers with a healthy understanding of their limitations. He wants to educate people to be aware of the cultural demands that are upon them and how they came to be. Then he offers guidance to help people live with a healthy margin.

CHAPTER 15: Hearing your calling

The Catalyst Leader by Brad Lomenick
Challenge level: Easy
This book (the first of two leadership books Lomenick has written) is an easy read for those beginning leadership. Lomenick is one of the organisers of the Catalyst Conference and is well positioned and networked to write on leadership. He offers a helpful overview of what leadership is about and what to be aware of as a leader.

The Making of a Leader by Robert Clinton
Challenge level: Mid–hard
Bobby Clinton, as he's affectionately known, is a leader of leaders. For years he has been leading leaders and studying leadership. This work is profound and a very helpful overview of the entire life cycle of a leader. Clinton writes so that people might know what to expect and focus on achieving all that they are positioned to effect.

CHAPTER 16: Embracing 'chair time'

Too Busy Not to Pray by Bill Hybels
Challenge level: Easy
I discuss this book in chapter 1. If prayer is not a strength for you, read this book. It will inspire and excite you about meeting with God every day and loving every minute of it. Hybels shares openly about his prayer journey and you will become more and more excited to pray as you read it.

The Life You've Always Wanted: Spiritual Disciplines for Ordinary People by John Ortberg
Challenge level: Easy
Ortberg seeks to make ancient spiritual disciplines as accessible as possible to everyone who would dare to lead. This would be a good entry-level book for someone looking to explore spiritual disciplines.

Spiritual Disciplines Handbook: Practices That Transform Us by Adele Ahlberg Calhoun
Challenge level: Easy
This book is a great resource. It covers a very wide range of spiritual disciplines and presents them in a very accessible fashion. A cross between a text book, guide book, reference book and how-to manual, it's a great resource to pick and choose from to resource you when you need it.

Loving God by Chuck Colson
Challenge level: Easy–mid
Colson writes to shake the church from its complacency and call it back to paying the price to serve and follow Christ. This book beckons its readers to more of what Christianity truly is and how to embrace it for all it's worth. With powerful stories, the book is a classic that will move you.

Gospel: Recovering the Power that Made Christianity Revolutionary by JD Greear
Challenge level: Mid
This book is a quest to recover the grace that the Gospel offers. Christianity is the response to a gift of grace that cannot be earned and no amount of work or effort will ever be able to secure. It is a gift of God that Greear is intent on assuring his readers know.

Celebration of Discipline by Richard Foster
Challenge level: Mid–exciting
Foster names 13 disciplines and then superbly and with great conviction walks you through how to develop these inner disciplines and entrench them into your life. His work is the book to go to when investigating spiritual disciplines.

The Spirit of the Disciplines by Dallas Willard
Challenge level: Hard (all of Willard's books are a deep read but incredibly rewarding)
This book takes a different angle than Foster's *Celebration of Discipline* by offering brilliant insight and compelling reasons to pursue God through a disciplined, holy life. Willard starts from the big picture and works in toward the detail.

Further resources

* * *

These resources will help you cultivate your potential to become an Anonymous Leader, by nurturing Christlike character in your life. You would be foolish, however, to assume that just reading the books and studying the material is enough. If you are a leader you need to lead something and someone! At the same time, you need to develop a rhythm of spending time with Jesus on a daily basis. Bringing together what Jesus is saying to you, while leading people and stretching what you already know, will see wisdom, integrity, humility, security and resilience flourish in your life

Of these five vital leadership components, you'll likely feel accomplished in some more than others. It is important you treat each of the five with equal respect and do what you need to do to move each attribute to the centre of the platform.

To achieve this, perhaps you need to enrol in some formal Bible study through a college, enter into an intentional discipleship course, arrange to have a spiritual advisor or mentor, ensure that you are in regular worship and regularly worshipping with that community, arrange times of extended solitude and self-reflection, or participate in a guided spiritual retreat. These are all options available for you to participate in and so respect the platform you have been gifted with. Any of these options, and others not mentioned, are excellent avenues to pursue in order to align the five components of leadership with the heart and mind of Christ, and see your influence become aligned to God's.

ACKNOWLEDGEMENTS

THIS BOOK WAS road-tested by some wonderful friends and excellent leaders, and their insights, wisdom and advice have benefitted this work no end. Thank you to the following who spent considerable time on this project with me: Craig Bailey, Dean Brookes, Stu Cameron, Jonathon Davies, Julian Dunham, Michael Hands, Graham Humphris, Phil McCallum, Neale Meredith, Philip Mutzelberg, Geoff Snook, Dale Stephenson and Ori Zacher.

Thanks also to Brad Beer – without your prompting to write this, I would not have struck the first key. Thank you for your guidance, friendship, encouragement and for leading the way.

And to my designer, Craig Hindman, and my social platform guru, Ori Zacher. Your friendship, generosity and patience have brought much to this project and my life. Thank you!

Finally, to my editor, Charlotte Duff, and publishing aficionado, Michael Hanrahan – thank you for all the guidance, encouragement and grace you have given me throughout this journey.

WHAT'S NEXT?

REVIEWS ARE GOLD to authors. If you have found this book helpful, please consider leaving an honest review on www.amazon.com. To do this simply open a free account on Amazon (it takes three minutes if you don't already have one). Then search for *The Anonymous Leader*, click on the book title, then click on the customer reviews link (just below the title) and finally click 'Write a customer review.' I would be so appreciative if you would help me in this way.

I would also love to hear from you if you have any feedback about the book, questions that have arisen for you, stories about how you are living this out or unfortunate spelling errors that eluded our team. PLEASE send me an email at ralph@ralphmayhew.com.

To read more of what I've written and what I have planned for the future, visit www.ralphmayhew.com for all the latest news.

You can find me on Facebook at www.facebook.com/ralph.mayhew or on Twitter @RalphMayhew. If you'd like to connect or if I can help you, please don't hesitate to make contact.

More copies of this book or the Anonymous Leader Workbook can be purchased at www.theanonymousleader.com. If you are outside of Australia go to www.amazon.com to purchase the book. The eBook and soon to be released audio book are also available through www.amazon.com.

If you write on leadership and would like to discuss partnering with me, please email me on leader@ralphmayhew.com. I'd be thrilled to hear from you.

Finally, for some fun, post a photo on social media (Facebook, Instagram or Twitter) of you holding the book (with a big thumbs up), using the hashtag #anonymousleader. It would be great to see whose hands the book ends up in.

ABOUT THE AUTHOR

RALPH MAYHEW IS married to Lyndal and together they have a two-year-old daughter with another child on the way. He serves as a pastor in an Associate capacity at Newlife Uniting Church on the Gold Coast (www.church.nu), where he develops leaders, pastors young adults and oversees strategic initiatives and the Generational Ministries.

Ralph understands what it means to intentionally influence and empower people, enabling them to achieve their goals. Over the last 18 years he has led emerging, developing and seasoned leaders in and out of church settings. He is just completing his Masters in Christian Leadership and has two other bachelor degrees to his name (one in theology) as well as an Advanced Diploma in Ministry.

Ralph has been writing on the subject of Christian leadership for over ten years. He has an entrepreneurial spirit and loves to create – and encourage those who are doing the same. He loves people and lives to see them fulfil their God-given potential.

www.ingramcontent.com/pod-product-compliance
Lightning Source LLC
Chambersburg PA
CBHW050530300426
44113CB00012B/2029